NEWS FROM A RADIANT FUTURE

SOVIET PORCELAIN

from the Collection of Craig H. and Kay A. Tuber

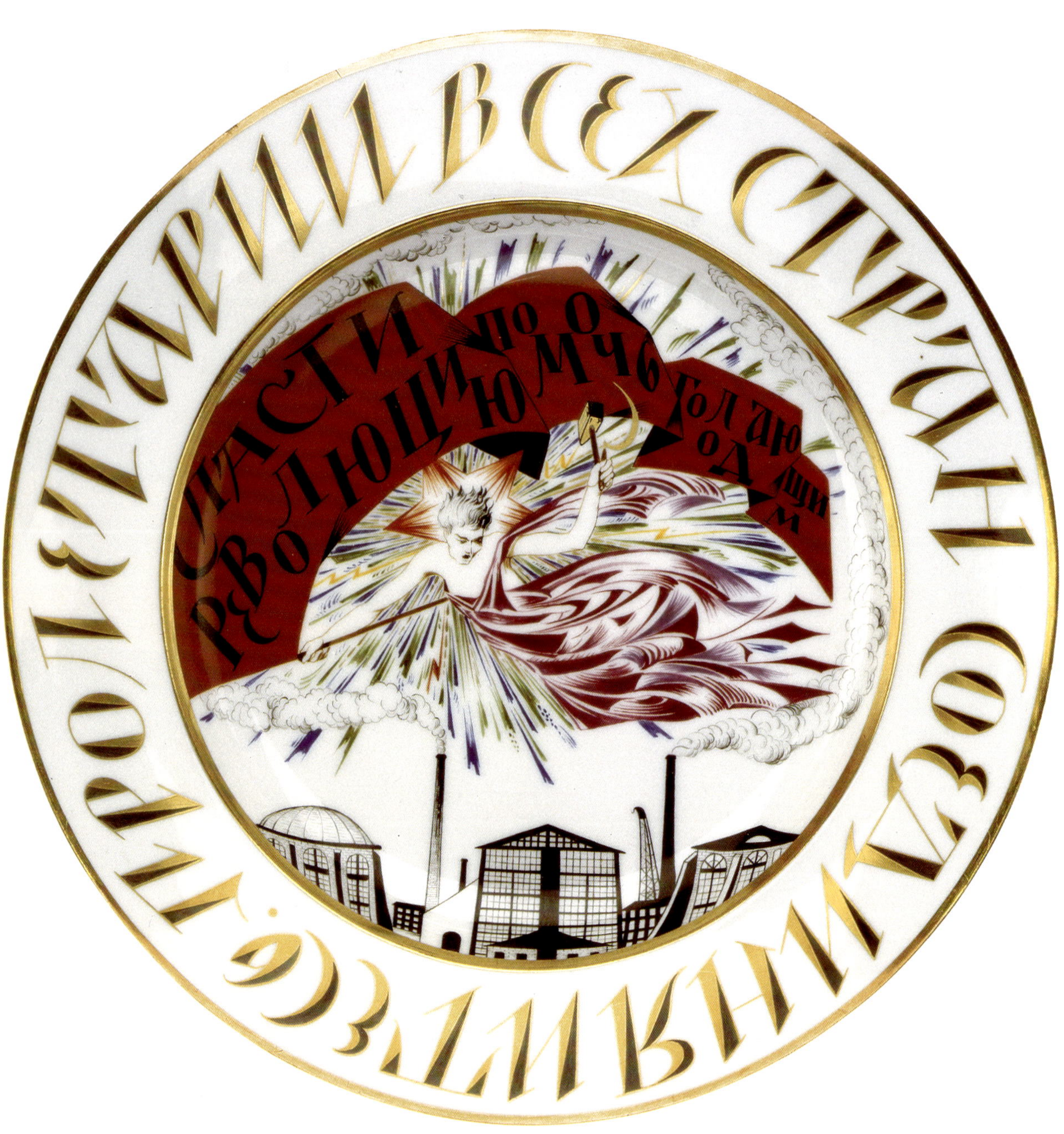

NO. 37

Rudol'f Vil'de

Plate, 1922

SOVIET PORCELAIN

from the Collection of Craig H. and Kay A. Tuber

Ian Wardropper, Karen Kettering,
John E. Bowlt, Alison Hilton

THE ART INSTITUTE OF CHICAGO

This catalogue accompanies the exhibition
**News from a Radiant Future:
Soviet Porcelain from the Collection
of Craig H. and Kay A. Tuber**
curated by Ian Wardropper
with the assistance of Karen Kettering

The Art Institute of Chicago
October 25, 1992–January 31, 1993

**The George R. Gardiner Museum at the
Royal Ontario Museum, Toronto**
March 6, 1994–July 31, 1994

The Minneapolis Institute of Arts
February 12, 1996–May 12, 1996

Susan F. Rossen, *Executive Director of Publications*
David Krasnow, *Editor*
Katherine Houck Fredrickson, *Senior Production
    Manager*
Ann Wassmann, *Senior Graphic Designer,
    Department of Graphic Services and Reproductions*
Christopher Gallagher, *Manager of Quality Control,
    Department of Imaging and Technical Services*

Typeset by Toby Zallman, Z...Art & Graphics
Printed at Rohner Printing Company, Chicago, Illinois
Reprinted in 1996 at C & C Offset Printing Co.,
Hong Kong.

This volume is the second in an ongoing series of
exhibition catalogues of European decorative arts
and sculpture at the Art Institute. The first, *Eighteenth-
Century English Pottery: Selections from the Collection
of Harry A. Root,* was published in 1991.

Front cover: Mikhail Adamovich, *Plate*, 1922 (no. 4).

ISBN: 0-86559-106-7

Table of Contents

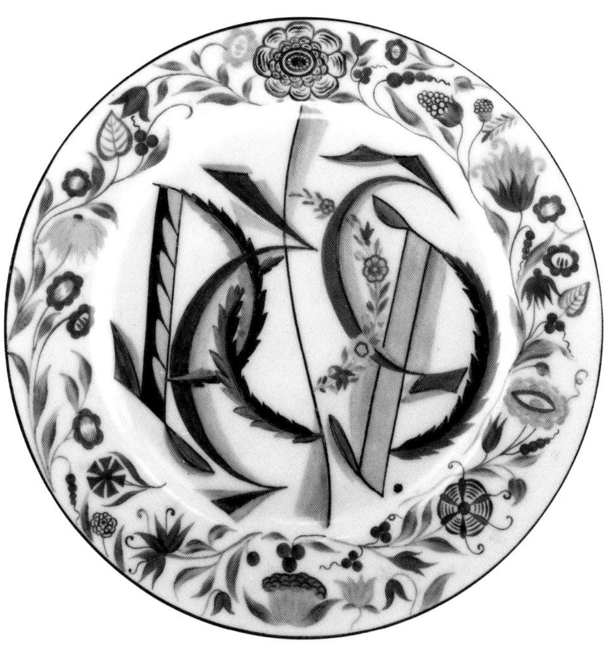

Editorial Note

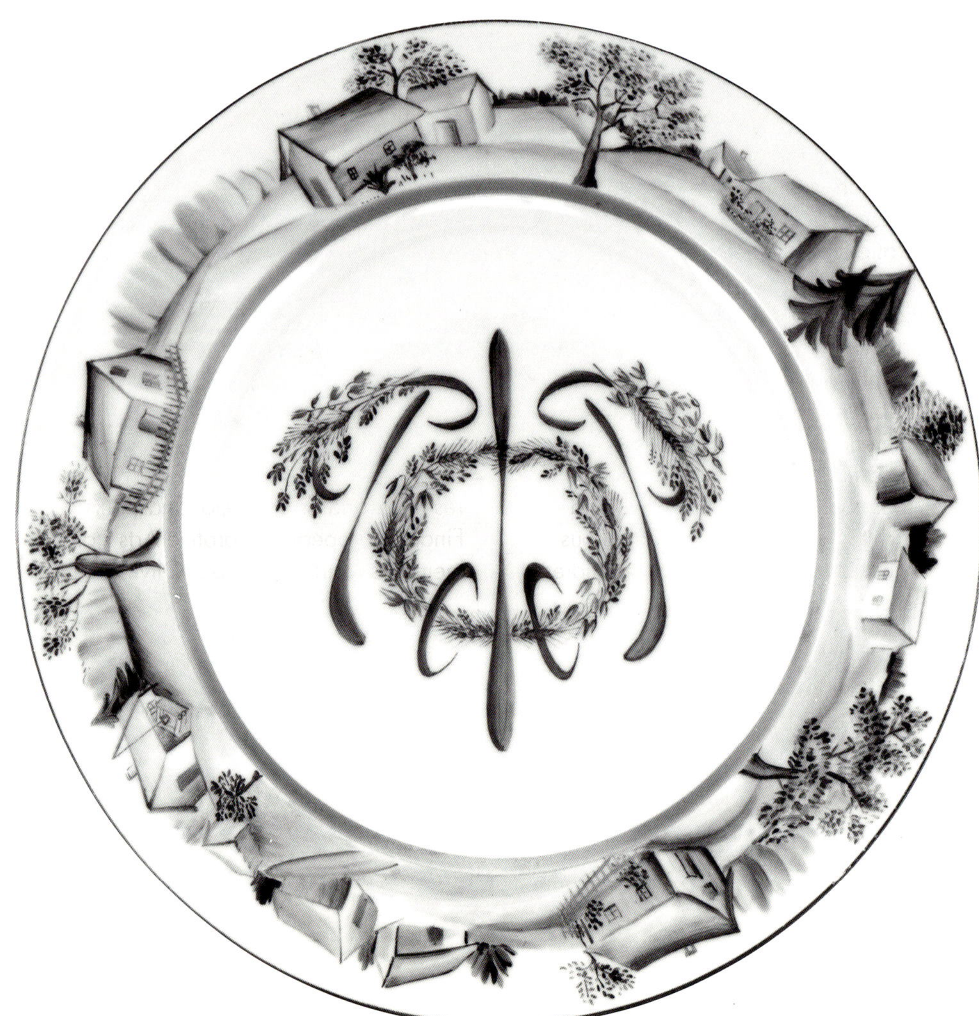

Russian names have been transliterated from the Cyrillic alphabet according to the Library of Congress system, with soft signs represented by an apostrophe (e.g., Dan'ko). Exceptions have been made where another transliteration is widely accepted (e.g., Tchaikovsky); two spellings are given in some cases—e.g., Lansere (Lancéray). In citations, the spelling as published has been retained. The names of Saint Petersburg, once Petrograd (1914–24) and then Leningrad (1924–91), have been used according to context; the present name has been used for general discussion. Likewise, the names Imperial (1744–1917) and State (1917–25) have been used for Russia's preeminent porcelain factory by context. (The factory was redesignated the Lomonosov State Porcelain Factory in 1925; this name has not been used). Dates before February 14, 1918, when the Soviet government's calendar reform took place, are given in the Julian or Old Style calendar, with the Gregorian date following in parentheses.   **D.H.K.**

NO. 22
Elizaveta Berngardovna
Rozendorf
*Plate,*1920

In a 1925 article on the post-Revolutionary production of the State Porcelain Factory in Leningrad, the ceramic artist Elena Dan'ko described the factory's wares as "news from a radiant future." The phrase conveys the promise that the plates' bold slogans and artistic excellence held for the fledgling state. Yet, since the porcelain used for this enterprise consisted mainly of blanks left over from imperial commissions, these plates are also survivors from Russia's past. Elucidating the meanings implicit in these objects—future promise, past elegance, present struggle—is the purpose of this exhibition, the first in this country to present Soviet porcelain from the first decade after the Revolution.

We are particularly grateful to Craig and Kay Tuber for agreeing to display their collection and for their generous financial support of this publication. The Tubers' enthusiasm for this art form nourished our preparations at every turn.

Karen Kettering, whose doctoral dissertation concerns the State Porcelain Factory, has dedicated two years to this project; her research skills and organizational ability are the armature on which this exhibition was built.

In addition to their informative contributions to this catalogue, John Bowlt and Alison Hilton gave advice on numerous questions. Other experts in Soviet studies helped shape this volume. Andrew Wachtel of Northwestern University checked the texts for accuracy of transliterations; John Bushnell, also of Northwestern, answered many historical and literary questions. Julie Hessler of the University of Chicago provided useful information. Katrina Taylor and Anne Odom of the Hillwood Museum were most helpful in obtaining information and photographs of works in their collection. Raymond Piper generously shared information about and photographs of works in his extraordinary personal collection of imperial Russian ceramics. Larisa Karagodina,

chief curator of the porcelain section, and several other curators of the Kuskovo Museum in Moscow were most accommodating in allowing us access to their rich collections of Russian and Soviet ceramics. Leon J. Dalva, Jr., of Dalva Brothers in New York, helpfully provided an illustration and information. We are particularly grateful to Nina Lobanov-Rostovsky for reviewing the catalogue entries. Responsibility for attribution, however, rests with the exhibition organizers.

Members of the staff of the Art Institute have aided this project with their usual high standards of professionalism. Chief among them are David Krasnow, who expertly edited this difficult subject, and Chris Gallagher, who skillfully photographed the entire collection. Ann Wassmann conceived the design and Kathy Fredrickson supervised the production of the catalogue. The Registrar's office was helpful in keeping track of the Tuber collection over the long period in which it has been in our care, and Pam Stuedemann was indispensable in coordinating the photography. Barbara Hall and Susie Schnepp of the Conservation Department assessed works in the collection. Interns Katherine Westerbeck and Megan Morrison aided us in preliminary research and organizational aspects. Finally, European Decorative Arts staff members Marilyn Conrad, Olivia White, Kirsten Darnton, Jane Neet, Tony Sigel, Bill Gross, and Heidi O'Neill were a constant source of support for both the exhibition and this catalogue.

I.W.

Introduction: Bolshevik Propaganda and the State Porcelain Factory

KAREN KETTERING, *Northwestern University*

The elegantly decorated Soviet porcelain wares in the Craig H. and Kay A. Tuber Collection are a paradox. They seem to epitomize the aristocratic culture the Bolsheviks sought to expunge from Russian society. Were these plates once the possessions of the nobility, appropriated for the common people? Were they the dinnerware of the Russian populace after the Revolution? Why would plates, cups, or vases have been considered effective sites from which to proclaim the slogans of the new state?

The works produced at the State Porcelain Factory in Petrograd are the product of the trying situation the Soviet government faced after the Revolution. World War I had seriously depleted the country's comparatively limited resources. The Bolshevik Party, having come to power suddenly from a minority position, was faced with the task of winning over the populace of a huge country; they recognized that they could transform Russian society only by convincing the Russian people of the value of their goals. The unexpected rise of the Bolsheviks and the questionable stability of their rule in the first few years made propaganda essential to the success of the October Revolution. Although the history of the early Soviet Union is thoroughly recounted in an exhaustive body of literature, a brief summary of the events may be helpful.

The power of the Romanov dynasty and its last tsar, Nicholas II, began to unravel in February 1917. Exhausted by the deprivations experienced during World War I and increasingly concerned about supplies of food, large groups of workers struck in Petrograd on February 23 (March 8), while women marched for bread. Petrograd, the capital of the Russian empire, had experienced periodic strikes throughout the first two months of 1917, and the tsar and his ministers expected that this incident too would pass. As the strikes continued over the next few days, however, troops sent to disperse the crowds instead joined them. Unrest spread to Moscow, the nation's second city, on March 2 (March 15). Nicholas soon abdicated both his own position and that of his son, Tsarevich Alexei, in favor of his brother, the Grand Duke Michael. But Michael refused the office, and the monarchy was effectively ended.

The February Revolution succeeded because elite and middle-class members of Russian society did not support Nicholas when unrest among the military and working class threatened his rule. The structure

FIGURE 1

Natan Al'tman, *design for the decoration of the General Staff Building in Petrograd,* pen and ink with watercolor, 1918. See cat. no. 7. The banners read, on the left, "Land to the workers," and on the right, "Factories to the workers."

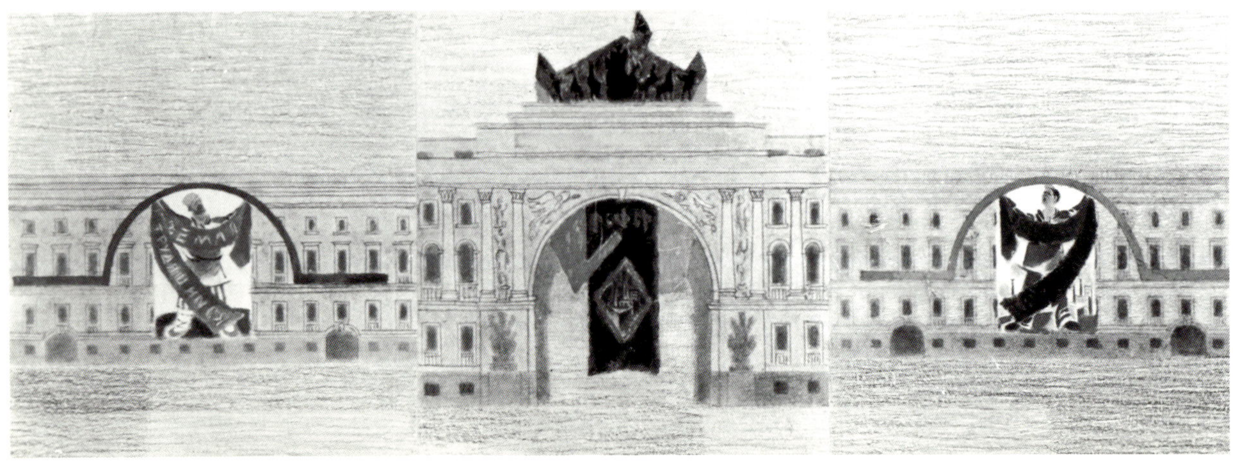

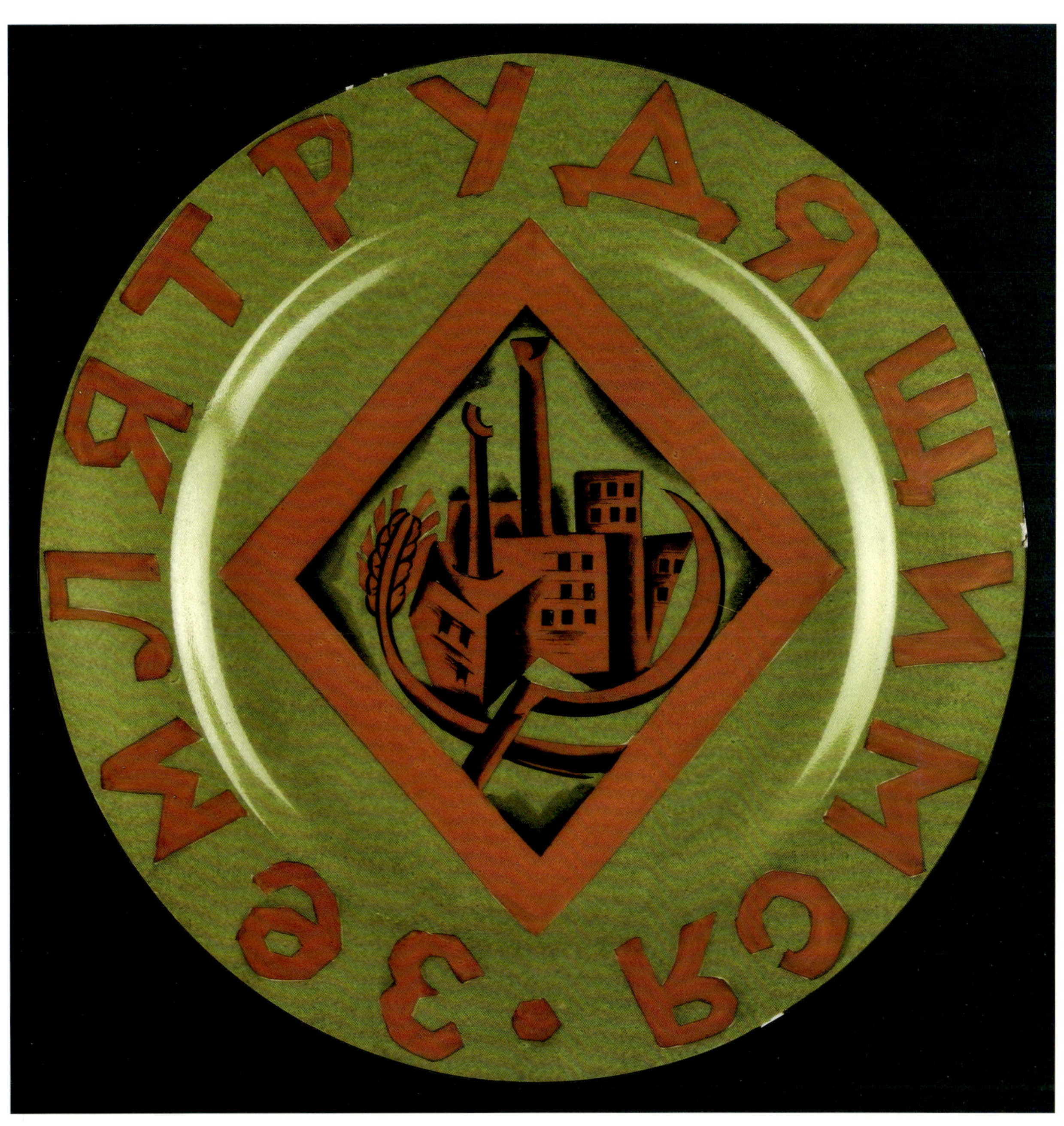
ЗЕМЛЯ ТРУДЯЩИМСЯ

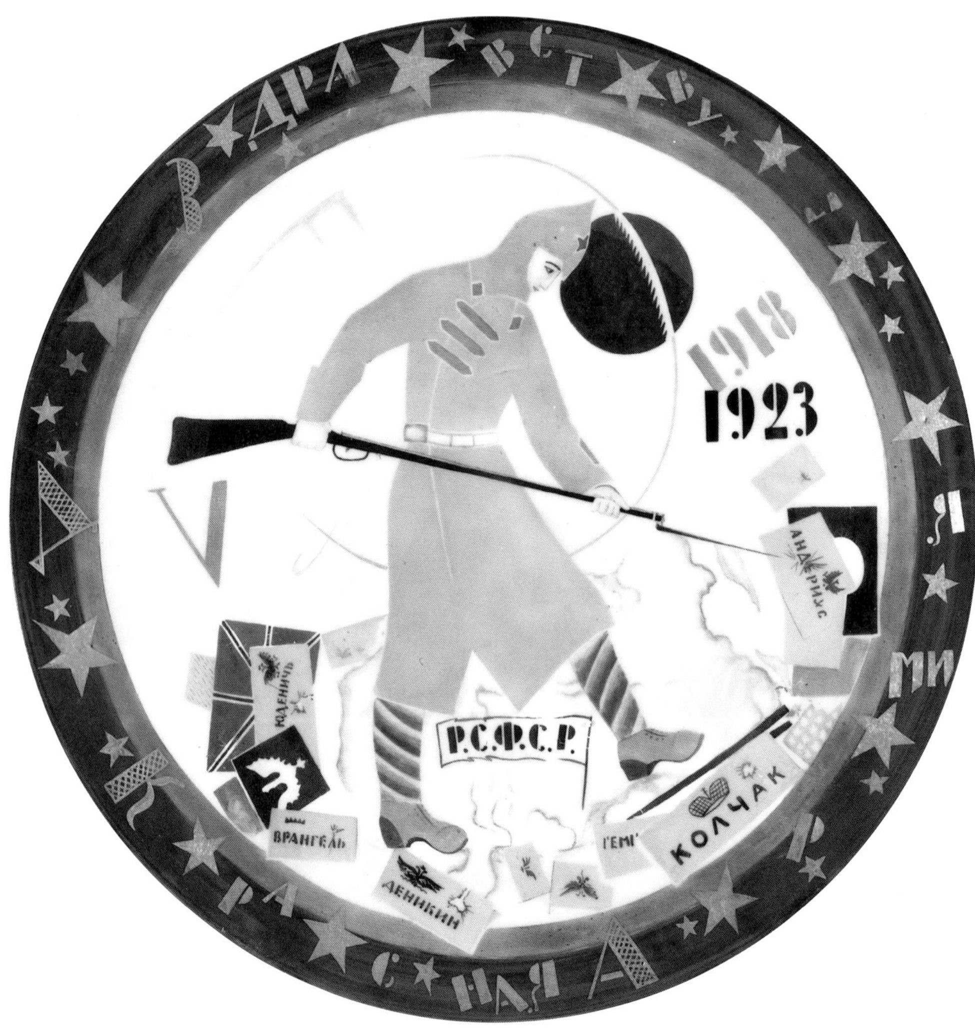

NO. 6

Mikhail Adamovich

Plate called "The Fifth Anniversary of the Red Army," 1923

of the post-monarchical government reflected these two broad power blocs. After the February Revolution, power was in theory shared by a Provisional Government and the Petrograd Soviet of Workers' and Soldiers' Deputies. This structure was to stay in place until elections were held and a Constituent Assembly had drafted a new constitution that would shape a Russian liberal democracy.

Shortly after the monarchy's demise, the leaders of the Bolshevik Party began to return from the exile imposed on them at the outbreak of World War I. Vladimir Lenin, head of the party, and twenty other revolutionary leaders, including Grigorii Zinov'ev (see cat. no. 42), arrived at Petrograd's Finland Station on April 3 (April 16). Standing atop an armored car, Lenin delivered the "April Theses," his assessment of the political situation and plan of action.

His arguments, which radically revised Marxist theory, stunned other Party members. Although Marx had written that a proletarian revolution—the passage of all state power and the means of production into the hands of the proletariat—is predicated upon the completion of a bourgeois revolution and the establishment of capitalism, Lenin argued that the Russian proletariat should not have allowed state power to pass into the hands of the bourgeoisie in February. Though capitalism had by no means been entrenched throughout imperial Russia, the workers and soldiers of Petrograd, he said, had achieved revolutionary consciousness. Lenin believed that Russia was now in a transitional phase in which the proletariat needed to wrest control away from the bourgeois Provisional Government.

Lenin's assessment was reinforced by the great support that his call for proletarian revolution found among urban workers; the Party grew from a few thousand members in February to 350,000 by the time of the October Revolution.[1] The Party's growth during these months indicated a widespread belief that the rule of the Provisional Government would differ little from that of the monarchy. This distrust resulted in another period of unrest and demonstrations known as the July Days.

A right-wing coup led by General Lev Kornilov, recently appointed Commander-in-Chief of the Russian Army, was thwarted by the concerted efforts of Petrograd workers; on August 31 (September 13), fearing the possibility of further right-wing action, delegates to the Petrograd Soviet elected the Bolsheviks to a majority position under the leadership of Leon Trotsky. Bolshevik discussions of insurrection became a reality on October 24 (November 6), the evening before the meeting of the Second Congress of Soviets. The Military-Revolutionary Committee of the Petrograd Soviet seized key points in the city, including the Winter Palace, where the Provisional Government kept offices. At the October 25 (November 7) meeting, delegates voted to transfer all power to the soviets, with administrative power passing to a Council of People's Commissars headed by Lenin, with Trotsky as foreign minister.

The Bolshevik position was dangerous. Although they gained control of Petrograd and Moscow by the end of October, central authority had collapsed throughout the rest of the country. Russia was still embroiled in World War I, and counter-revolutionary armies were forming under the command of tsarist generals. The Civil War had begun by the summer of 1918. Without the resources to assert power, the Bolsheviks could only gain control of the country if they were able to win over the Russian people.

They were uniquely prepared for this effort. Marx had written that the working class would achieve class consciousness (leading to revolution) only through their experiences under capitalism; Lenin held that the working class required intellectuals of a vanguard party to lead them to this consciousness.[2] The Bolshevik Party had long been engaged in propaganda, edu-

cating workers and soldiers to recognize that the party represented their political interests. Bolshevik leaders felt that the culturally "backward" state of the Russian people was the greatest obstacle to the creation of socialism. As Trotsky summarized the problem:

The bourgeoisie [of the French Revolution] came into power fully armed with the culture of its time. The proletariat, on the other hand, comes into power fully armed only with the acute need of mastering culture.[3]

The task of enculturating the masses fell to the People's Commissariat of Enlightenment (Narodnyi Kommissariat Prosveshcheniia), called Narkompros. Lenin selected Anatolii Lunacharskii, a long-time party member recognized for his cultural enthusiasms and already well connected to Russian literary circles, to head this important government department. Not only was Narkompros responsible for public education at all levels, as well as child welfare, but it also controlled existing art institutions that had formerly been under the aegis of the tsar's Palace Ministry. Thus, among all its other duties, Narkompros was responsible for the imperial theaters and the Academy of Arts, and for guarding the cultural property of the state. The former Imperial Porcelain Factory, renamed the State Porcelain

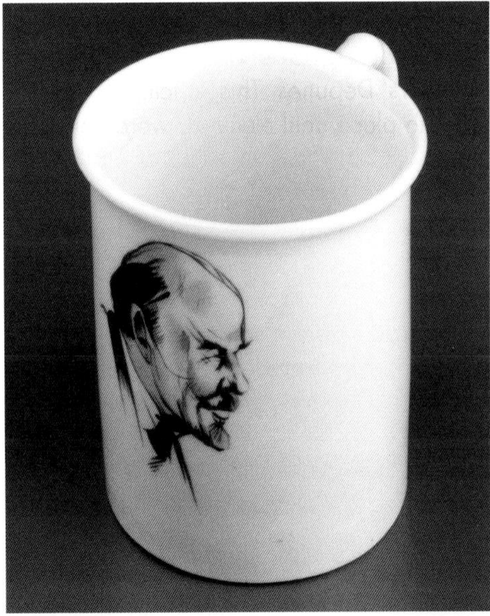

NO. 43
Cup, c. 1924/28

Factory after the February Revolution, came under the control of Narkompros's Fine Arts Department (Otdel Izobrazitel'nykh Iskusstv, or IZO) in March 1918. After the October Revolution, the former administrators had departed en masse, and by January the factory council barely managed to convince the workers to keep the factory running.[4] The factory's integration into Narkompros provided it an avenue to acquire materials and for its employees to draw pay.

The relationship between the State Porcelain Factory and Narkompros explains many of the early themes of the factory's wares. As part of its responsibility for education and the arts, Narkompros was charged with the administration of the nationwide literacy campaign aimed at eradicating the problem of cultural "backwardness." With paper for poster production somewhat restricted, the large supply of unused blanks in the factory's storerooms, pressed but never decorated during the tsars' patronage, must have been recognized as a valuable resource. Now, new designs painted on plates, platters, and teacups promoted the campaign for literacy (see cat. no. 32), the efforts to help alleviate the starvation of the Volga famine (see cat. no. 37), or the political philosophy of the new government (see, e.g., cat. nos. 18, 31). Objects such as these were never put to conventional use, but were probably distributed and displayed like propaganda posters.

The initial propaganda orientation of the wares produced soon shifted when the government recognized the factory's potential for generating funds. As John E. Bowlt mentions in this volume, the factory was exporting porcelain by 1920. The next year, *Sredi kollektsionerov* (Among the collectors), a Moscow-based, anachronistic magazine for connoisseurs and collectors, happily announced that the factory's Petrograd store once again had tea services, platters, and figurines available for sale.[5] The factory even reproduced popular works of the imperial period, such as the "Peoples of Russia" series of statuettes (discussed by Ian Wardropper in this volume). Prices were steep, ranging from 20,000 to 300,000 rubles for teacups to 1,200,000 rubles for a tea service (when

the average monthly wage was less than 10,000 rubles). Such prices obviously made the objects available to very few, probably only the remnants of the capitalist bourgeoisie, in the Soviet Union.[6]

Although its production was relatively limited, the State Porcelain Factory left behind a rich legacy. In the objects in this catalogue, we have a record of the beginnings of a socialist iconography in the Soviet Union that was to develop through the following decades. Older imperial and folk styles and motifs continued as artists struggled to ascertain and meet the tastes of new patrons and a new regime. Works of the State Porcelain Factory chronicle the momentous events of the Revolution, the country's hopes for the future, and its disappointments.

NOTES

1. Sheila Fitzpatrick, *The Russian Revolution, 1917–1932* (Oxford and New York, 1982), p. 46.
2. See Peter Kenez, *The Birth of the Propaganda State: Soviet Methods of Mass Mobilization, 1917–1929* (Cambridge, England, 1985), pp. 1–17.
3. Leon Trotsky, *Literature and Revolution* (New York, 1957), p. 191.
4. P. A. Friken, "Zhizn' gosudarstvennogo farforovogo zavoda v 1917–22 gg.," in E. F. Gollerbakh and M. V. Farmovskii, eds., *Russkii khudozhestvennyi farfor: Sbornik statei o gosudarstvennom farforovom zavode* (Leningrad, 1924), p. 20.
5. "Pis'ma iz Petrograda," *Sredi kollektsionerov*, 1921, no. 10 (Nov.), p. 61.
6. For more information on prices and wages during this period, see Silvana Malle, *The Economic Organization of War Communism, 1918–1921* (New York, 1985); Alec Nove, *An Economic History of the U.S.S.R.* (London, 1969); and L. E. Hubbard, *Soviet Money and Finance* (London, 1936).

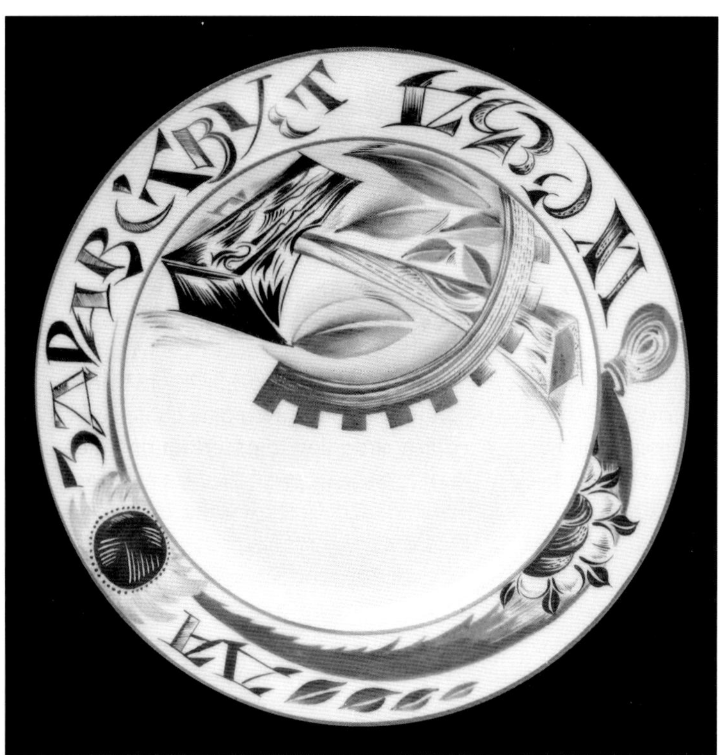

NO. 36
Rudol'f Vil'de
Plate, 1922

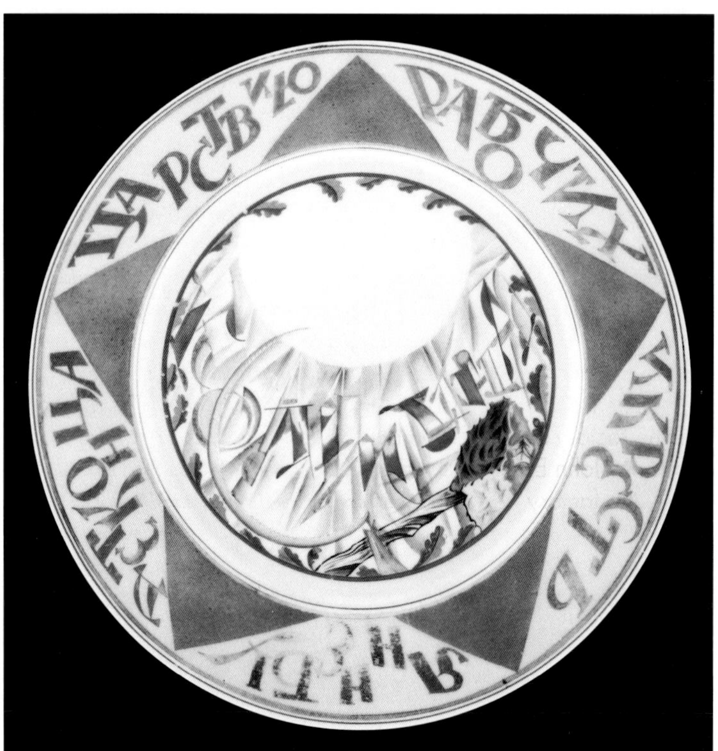

NO. 10
Sergei Chekhonin
Plate, 1920

Red Stars on White Plates: Soviet Propaganda Porcelain and the Tradition of Russian Imperial Ceramics

IAN WARDROPPER, *Eloise W. Martin Curator of European Decorative Arts and Sculpture, and Classical Art, The Art Institute of Chicago*

The avant-garde design and revolutionary slogans brandished by Soviet propaganda porcelain of the period 1918–27 proclaim it to be a new art form for the proletariat. Fixing the chants of street demonstrators and the ephemeral messages of their placards to elegant porcelain surfaces, the workers of the State Porcelain Factory in Petrograd (formerly the Imperial Porcelain Factory in Saint Petersburg) redirected the purpose of aristocratic tableware from the embellishment of banquets to the promotion of urgent social concerns. Unpainted, fired porcelain blanks in the factory storerooms, left over from past or prospective imperial commissions, were given over to artists working under Sergei Chekhonin. The imperial marks on the porcelain's undersides were so abhorrent to the new administration that at first Revolutionary painters blotted them out and added the cogwheel, hammer, and sickle symbol of the new factory (see the "Notes on Marks," pp. 88–89). A famous plate by Mikhail Adamovich (cat. no. 4) features the red star, symbol of the new government, blocking out the double-headed eagle of the tsars. Both the fronts and the undersides of these plates trace the tension between former and present patrons of the factory.

As radically new as these ceramic images appear, they were shaped by Russian ceramic history and depended on old-regime content as well as form. Though their style is shockingly modern compared to that which preceded it, the designers and painters who made them frequently borrowed techniques, motifs, ideas, and functions from the previous era. In some cases, this adoption of old manners was purposeful, subverting past custom to new causes; in others, it may have been unconscious gesture, habitually returning to established practice. In either case, the blanks found in the factory storage racks were not truly clean slates, wiped of all traces of previous use. The memory of old forms associated with them and two centuries of Russian porcelain production inevitably influenced the new painted decoration.

A precedent for the use of porcelain and faience to promote the ideals of a new political order existed in the French Revolution. Phrygian bonnets and the tricolor, slogans proclaiming "liberté, egalité, fraternité," symbolic roosters crowing vigilance, and cats facing off counterrevolutionary dogs were turned into decorative images in the Revolutionary spirit. Sèvres porcelain of this period often used forms that had been invented for the old regime, such as a service originally ordered for the dairy at Marie Antoinette's Rambouillet estate, while substituting emblems of the French Republic (see fig. 1). If most of these French ceramics appear tame beside the Russian ones created more than a century later, it may be because the efforts of the French factories at Sèvres and Nevers were sponsored individually, rather than by a concerted policy of the state. Napoleon recognized the value of regenerating industries devastated by war; he commissioned ceramics and textiles to stimulate the French economy as well as to buttress his political image with a carefully devised personal style. The relatively few examples of faience and porcelain fired in Revolutionary zeal were soon displaced by Empire ceramics, which continued the artistic traditions of the preceding century.[1]

The Bolsheviks scarcely wanted to create a life-style commensurate with that of the tsars. Their solution—to turn porcelain blanks into propaganda weapons—required a small-scale craft of hand-painted porcelain that existed alongside the large-scale production of ordinary ceramics. In the period 1918–27, the renewal of the State Porcelain Factory represented neither regeneration of industry nor mass produc-

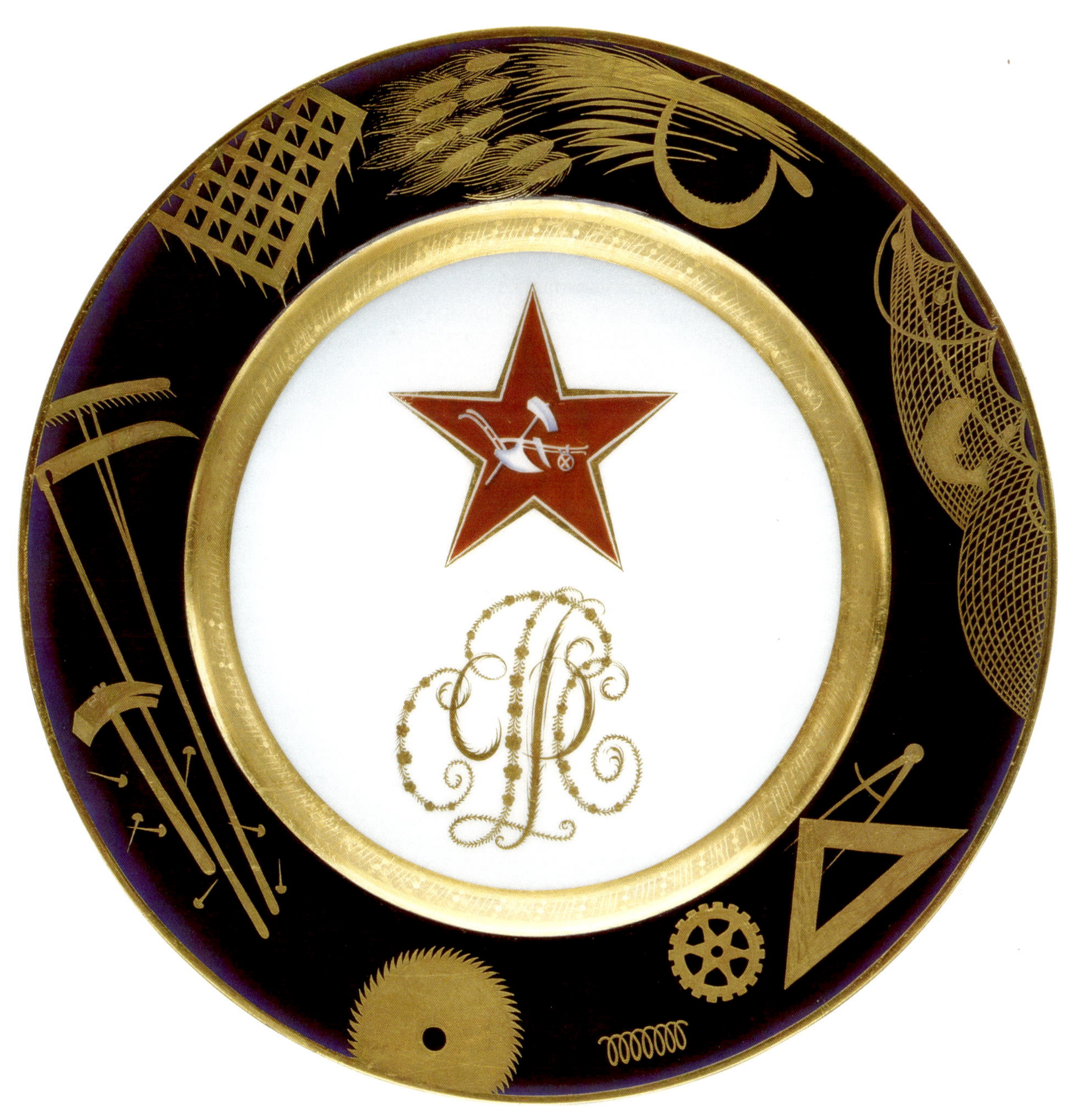

tion for the whole of society; rather, the workers in Petrograd simply did the best they could within the limitations of the time. Propaganda porcelain made good use of an available resource, the excellent-quality blanks, and put a relatively small number of painters and designers to work. The contradiction of these aims with the industrial orientation of the new state demonstrates the ambivalence toward craft after the Revolution. For many, craft was retrograde; but for others, it was a valued link to the peasantry.[2] These plates embody such mixed messages and shifting attitudes. Unlike post-Revolutionary France, the Soviet Union never returned to the production of porcelain on an imperial scale and finesse.

Well before the French Revolution, the history of Russia's fascination with porcelain closely followed developments in Germany and France. Inspired by imported Chinese porcelain, Europeans made repeated attempts to create their own versions of this fine oriental ware. The first successful firing of hard-paste porcelain took place at the Meissen factory in Germany about 1708 under the arcanist Johann Friedrich Böttger. By 1716, Peter the Great had received a service of Böttger's porcelain.[3] But the hard-won secret of manufacture was jealously guarded by the Saxon enterprise, and only in the mid-1740s did Dmitrii Vinogradov, under the sponsorship of Tsarina Elizabeth I, succeed in creating hard-paste porcelain from native clays in Saint Petersburg. One of the first sustained results of his labor was the "Private Service of Her Majesty" produced for Elizabeth about 1756. With its swirling trellis pattern of flowers and applied floral bouquets, it is clearly indebted to the basketwork borders ornamenting Meissen of the 1730s, and it resembles, as well, English patterns, such as Derby, of the 1750s.[4]

Under Catherine the Great, the Imperial Porcelain Factory expanded and private factories flourished. After visiting the Imperial Factory in 1763, Catherine ordered that skilled modelers and painters be brought from Austria, Germany, and France to improve quality and enliven design.[5] Eventually, the assimilation of foreign patterns was systematically promoted as the factory required each foreign workman to train two Russians.[6] Despite the

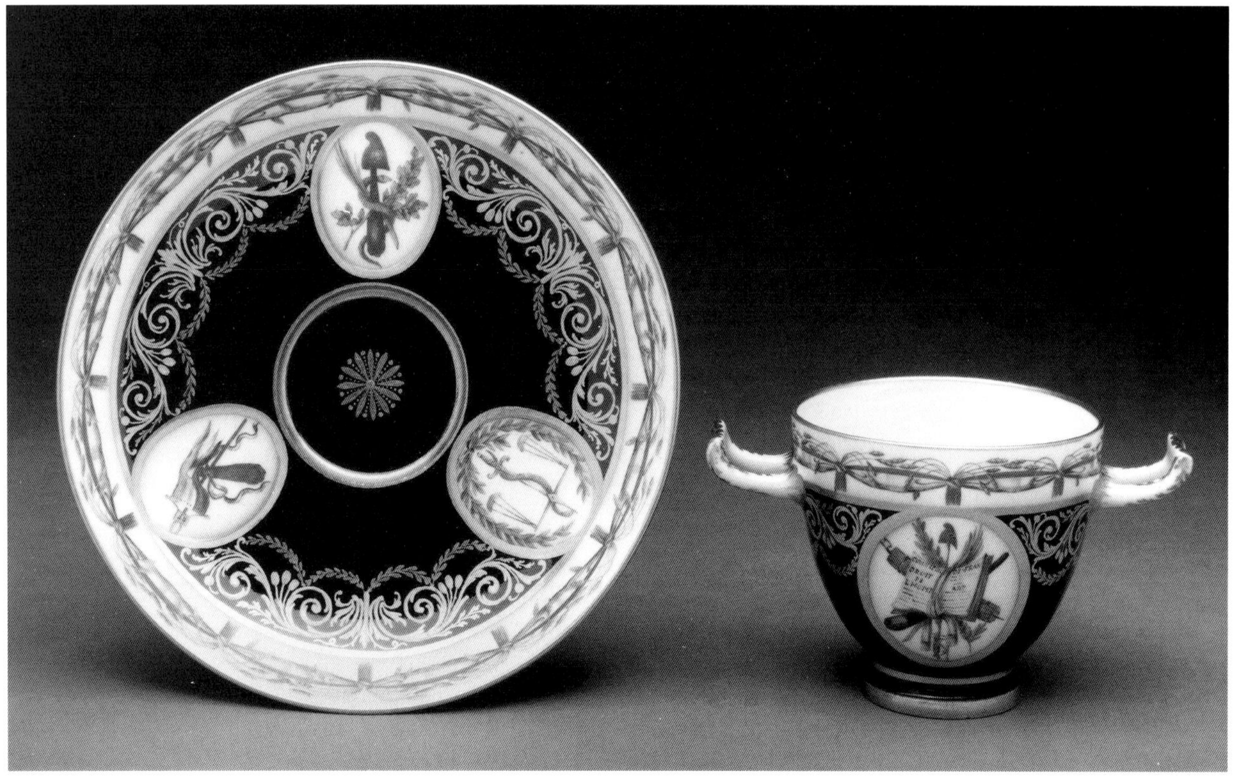

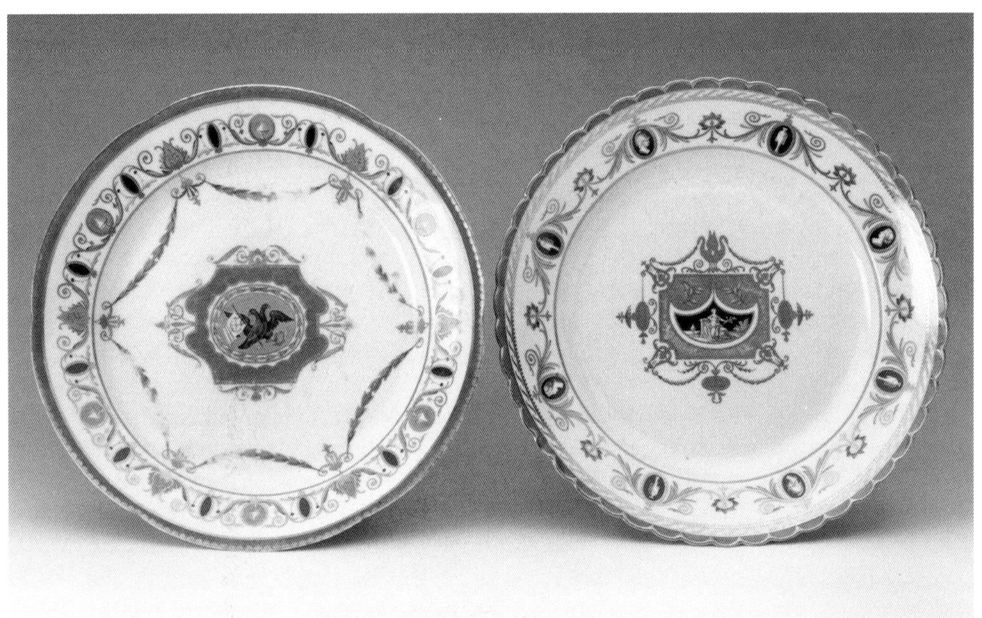

prominence of foreign craftsmen, the high-key coloring and unusual forms of the porcelain they produced in Saint Petersburg had a distinctively Russian flavor. Immigrant artists may even have been more attuned to traditional Russian designs than their native counterparts, long trained to look west for the latest fashion; and German-born Catherine encouraged the use of native styles in her adopted country to reinforce her acceptance by her subjects.

These opposing currents—foreign forms and native content—can be seen in the Arabesque Service of 1784 and the Yachting Service, which Catherine probably used with it (see fig. 2). Fashionably neoclassic, with severe organization and motifs culled from recently excavated frescoes at Pompeii and Herculaneum, the Arabesque Service centered on scenes of industry and the arts and was ringed by classical portraits. The Yachting Service featured the emblem of the merchant marine, the imperial eagle holding a laurel wreath with a flag of crowned anchors. Celebrating Russian naval victories, these services glorified their owner's reign.[7]

The most successful private factory founded in Catherine's reign was that of the Englishman Francis Gardner, officially established in 1766 and based in the village of Verbilki near Moscow.[8] The Gardner Factory's wares were purchased by a wide range of customers, including the imperial family, well into the nineteenth century. Its most famous porcelains were the order services, produced between 1778 and 1785. Commissioned by the imperial court, they were intended to honor the recipients of ceremonial orders, and were used at annual Winter Palace banquets held on the feast days of the saints for whom the orders were named.[9] First and highest of these, the Order of Saint Andrew, was first conferred in Moscow in 1699; recipients were members of the royal family, diplomats, and military commanders. Other orders initiated in the eighteenth century included that of Aleksandr Nevskii (see fig. 3), rewarding feats of arms, and of Saint George, for military bravery. The porcelain reproduced the orders' ribbons, embroidered badges, ceremonial chains, and mottoes, gracefully adapting these insignia to the centers and rims of plates and bowls.[10]

The high standard of quality set by the earliest Russian porcelain continued in the nineteenth century, even with the large volume of palace services and the increased production of the private factories. An 1806 tariff on imports provided economic protection and stimulated local production. While Russian designers kept an eye on Western fashions, ceramics developed a notably national style in this century. A

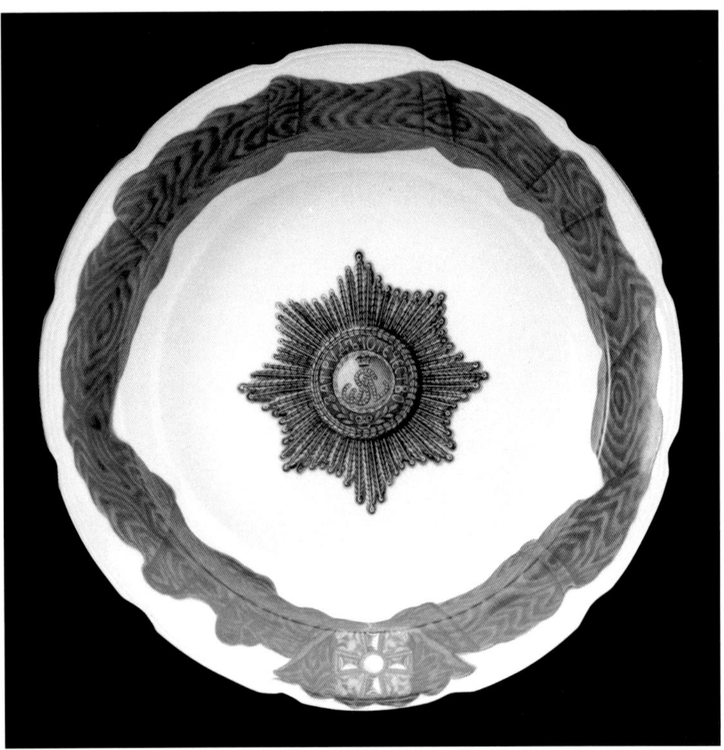

high point of the Imperial Factory production was the Gur'ev Service, 1809–17, named for the director of the tsar's Cabinet. A dinner, dessert, and tea service originally created for fifty place settings, the Gur'ev Service was later expanded to include 4,500 pieces. Brick red and gold, it is a celebration of Russian ethnic and cultural diversity (see fig. 4). Sculpted figural groups that support the centerpieces were modeled by Nikolai Pimenov to represent Russian peasant women. The centers of the plates depict scenes from folk life as well as country estates.[11]

The 1812 defeat of Napoleon's forces, often called the "Great Patriotic War," awakened a spirit of nationalism. Nascent slavophile sentiment, leary of Western influence, prompted artists to reflect their country's range of folk and ethnic identities in painting and architecture. The decorative arts mirrored this interest; one source for the decoration of the Gur'ev Service was the engraved illustrations of academician Johann Georgi's *Description of All the Peoples Inhabiting the State of Russia* (translated from German into Russian in 1776). Even before the images of folk life on the Gur'ev Service, statuettes of peas-

ants had been modeled by the Danish-born Jean Dominique Rachette, who joined the Imperial Factory in 1779.[12] Basing his studies on Georgi's historically accurate engravings, Rachette created a popular series of idealized statuettes of Russians (see fig. 5). By the early nineteenth century, Aleksei Venetsianov's images for *Volshebni fonar* (Magic lantern), a journal that first appeared in 1817,[13] fueled this long-standing Russian obsession with images of peasants, particularly in the output of the Popov Factory, which specialized in working-class figures. This tradition continued after the Revolution with a series of statuettes of the working class (not represented in the Tuber collection). A militaristic side of this nationalist mood is reflected in plates depicting the armed services, ranging from the cossacks on the Black Sea to the hussar regiments favored by the emperors. Some of these plates are based on albums Nicholas I commissioned to record his soldiers' uniforms (see fig. 6); others reproduce battle paintings or lithographs of army life. The French battle-scene painter Jacques François José Swebach was brought in to train Russian artists at the Imperial Porcelain Factory in 1815, and plates in this tradition were produced throughout the century.[14]

The Gur'ev Service was the last great Imperial Factory service created without a specific palace as destination. Subsequent services often matched the architectural decor or programmatic theme of the rooms they graced. The Gothic Service of 1831, for instance, with radiant colors based on stained-glass windows, was intended for the neomedieval Cottage Palace in Peterhof.[15] Nicholas I commissioned the Kremlin Service, 1837–38, for the rebuilt Grand Kremlin Palace (see fig. 7). This consciously antiquarian service was based on the gilt and enameled coronation plate of Tsar Alexei Mikhailovich. It was designed by the architect and archaeologist Fedor Solntsev, cataloguer of the Kremlin treasures and author of *Antiquités de l'Empire de Russie,* to be stylistically compatible with the architecture and the objects presented museologically in the palace. Other services by Solntsev, such as that of 1848 for Grand Duke Konstantin

Nikolaevich, adopted a Byzantine style with an interlacing pattern drawn from book illumination and metalwork and meant to evoke Russian Orthodox origins.[16]

The search for an identifiably Russian style led to the incorporation of patterns from rustic woodcarving and peasant cross-stitch embroideries. A neo-Russian style was deliberately chosen for export to America. The Kornilov Factory, founded in Saint Petersburg in 1835 and in production until the Revolution, chose Cyrillic inscriptions and other stylized motifs from native arts that could readily be identified as Russian when the firm shipped large numbers of pieces to the United States around the time of the World's Columbian Exposition in Chicago in 1893.[17] The emancipation of the serfs in 1861 closed a number of private factories that had depended on the cheap labor of serf-craftsmen. But the larger concerns—like the Kornilov and the Imperial Porcelain Factory—continued, sometimes consolidating as the Gardner Factory did with the Kuznetzov Combine in 1892 (surviving the Revolution as the Dmitrov Porcelain Factory).

Even this brief sketch of Russian porcelain of the eighteenth and nineteenth centuries attests to the wealth of tradition available to the revitalized factory in Petrograd. Clearly, too, Russian old-regime ceramics were not innocent of political motifs. As has been suggested, some of Catherine's services alluded to Russian naval might; the order services overtly honored national military prowess. The very establishment of porcelain factories in Russia was intended to

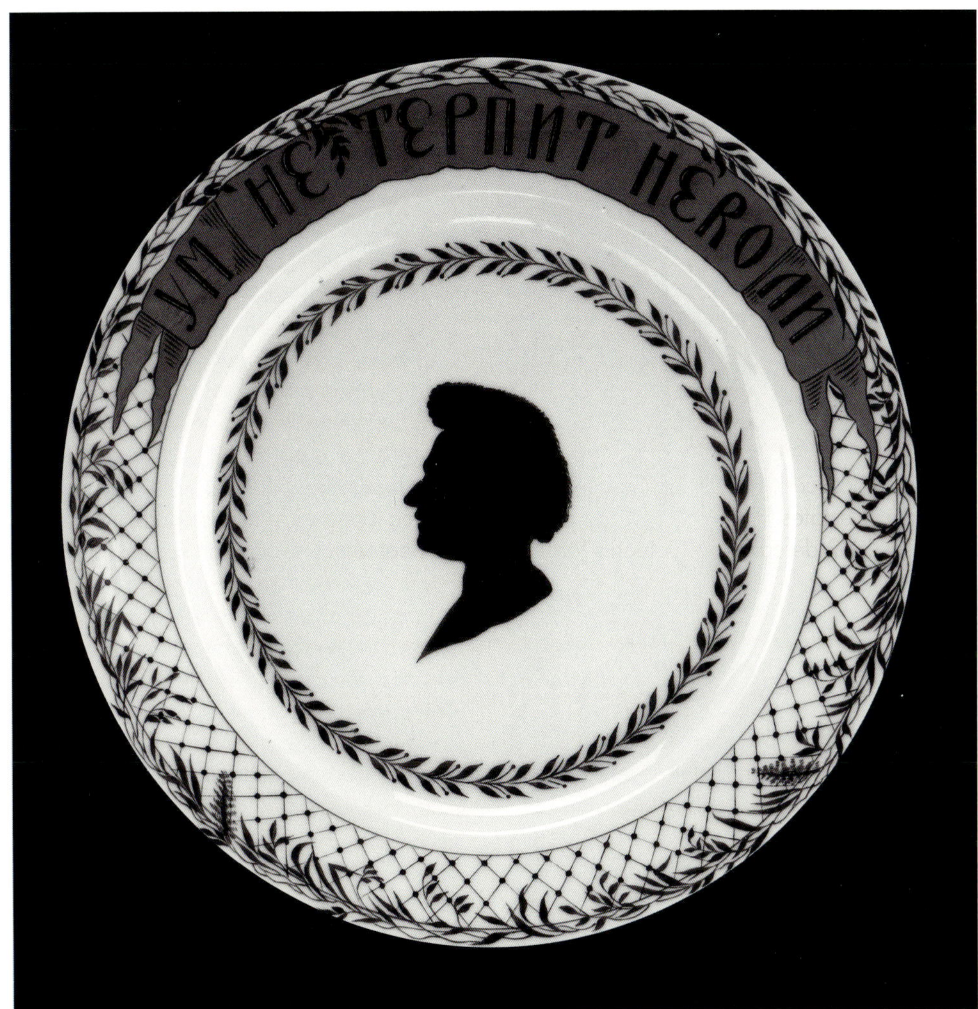

compete with the West, artistically and economically. Increasingly through the nineteenth century, ceramics celebrated ethnic diversity in folk scenes and championed national identity through native patterns and forms. In content, form, technique, and function, the propaganda porcelain of the early Soviet period only made manifest what had been latent in earlier examples.[18]

Two subjects for ceramic decoration that survived the change of regime were the military and peasant life. Although their implications changed radically after the Revolution, the ultimate aim of glorifying military might and rallying all regions of the nation remained substantially the same. Adamovich's "Fifth Anniversary of the Red Army" plate (cat. no. 6) echoes early nineteenth-century scenes of soldiers in combat and regiments on parade. The Red Army soldier bayoneting flags of the White generals and striding across a map of the Soviet Union is allegorical, in contrast to the precisely rendered cavalrymen in naturalistic landscape settings of nineteenth-century plates, but the idealization of the Russian soldier guarding the nation underlies both versions. Other Soviet plates, such

as Shchekotikhina-Pototskaia's 1921 "The Sailor Takes a Walk" (cat. no. 25), even carefully identify the uniform, here that of a Baltic Fleet sailor, in the "trooping of the regiment" spirit that characterizes the earlier plates. An obvious difference of approach is the valorization of the ordinary foot soldier in Soviet plates, rather than the tendency to depict the officer class in the earlier works. The theme of fraternization of military and civilians, so important to the collective efforts of the new nation, is also clearly marked in such works as a vase by Timorev (cat. no. 31), in which a sailor and a soldier link arms with a factory worker and a peasant.

Scenes from country life, such as nut peddlers and women in the traditional dress of Tashkent or Estonia, found on the Gur'ev Service, return in Shchekotikhina's lyrical renderings of peasant life, such as the "Wool Winders" (cat. no. 26). Absent is the formal context of the Gur'ev Service —the gilt, neoclassical palmetto borders and lavish size of the service—that distanced these genre scenes from their aristocratic users. They had ceased to represent the cataloguing of peasants, and instead celebrated practices rooted in the land with designs in the spirit of untutored handicraft. Of course, the relationship of Bolshevik leaders and avant-garde artists to peasants in the country had a remove of its own, and was rarely as familiar as the propaganda images implied. Even Shchekotikhina's apparently ingenuous affection for peasant culture was informed by research trips, as were Georgi's fact-finding journeys in the eighteenth century.

The retention of certain forms of decoration in post-Revolutionary ceramics has a clear political message. The tsars' double-headed eagle, usually the center of earlier services' decoration, was transmuted into the hammer and sickle, symbols of the workers' state. The tsars' initials, artfully embellished with flowers, concealed in gold links, or boldly abstracted as Cyrillic ciphers, are replaced by the initials R.S.F.S.R. (see, e.g., cat. no. 14) for the Russian Soviet Federal Socialist Republic (precursor to the U.S.S.R). The new designers took an old delight in seeking ways to elaborate or disguise the central motif, par-

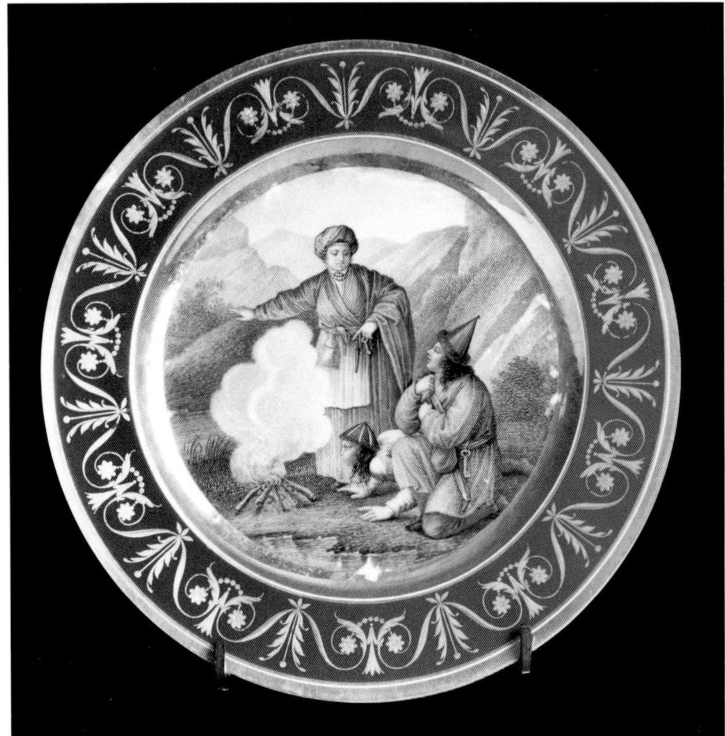

FIGURE 4

Imperial Porcelain Factory, *plate entitled "The Laplanders" from the Gur'ev Service,* porcelain, 1809/17. Collection of Patrick Daly on loan to the Hillwood Museum.

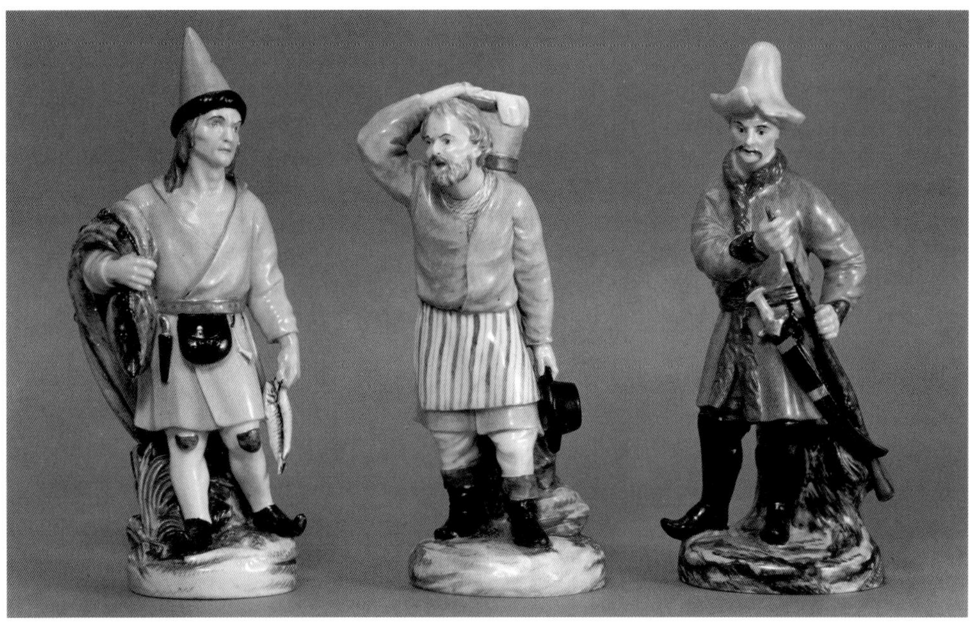

ticularly by tucking the curving sickle into the cavity of the plate or by merging these implements with letters or floral decoration. On the new ceramics as on the old, symbols of power are omnipresent, constant reminders of the political order.

Other trappings of the former regime were preserved to confer honor on heroes of the new state. Particularly notable is the use of ribbons, the prominent and unusual features of the order services of the Gardner Factory in the eighteenth century. Red or orange ribbons circling a plate were associated with the services for the Orders of Saint George or Aleksandr Nevskii, and thus with the high stature of the nobility. When the silhouette of Bolshevik Party leader Grigorii Zinov'ev is framed by such a ribbon (cat. no. 44), he is ennobled with the high honors of the new state. The red ribbon bordering the plate inscribed "1917–1921, 4 years" (cat. no. 13) implies that all the proletariat who participated in the efforts of these first years deserve recognition.

An abiding interest in inscriptions—phrases or proverbs incorporated into the design of a plate—also passes from old to new regime. Through mottoes on the order services such as "For love and country," "For service and valor," "For work and country," Russian ceramics urged viewers to practice high standards of conduct. Ceramic eggs, traditional gifts at Easter,

bore such legends as "Christ has risen." The Russian fondness for proverbs led to frequent inclusion of such sayings as "Do not eat the bread of others" in the neo-Russian style at the end of the nineteenth century; this exhortation corresponds directly to some post-Revolutionary subjects, like Adamovich's plate depicting ration cards with the slogan "He who does not work, does not eat" (cat. no. 4).[19] The prevalence of words on these plates, noted by John E. Bowlt in this volume, is a prime characteristic of Revolutionary ceramics. Yet the tendency to use ceramics as a podium for speech already had a long history in Russia.

Though the administration and staff of the factory turned over drastically following the Revolution, a number of prominent Soviet artists, like Zinaida Kobyletskaia, had worked there during previous regimes. Many techniques survived and were put to use in the new production. Adamovich's plate "The Red Star" (cat. no. 5) illustrates this well. In several important ways it capitalizes on old, highly refined techniques to promote the new aesthetics and ideology. The color scheme of gilt over a cobalt blue border with red and gold decoration in the white reserve is fundamentally the same as a number of imperial plates, such as one (fig. 8) that may be part of the coronation service of Alexander II.[20] Adamovich, who had been commissioned by the Greek gov-

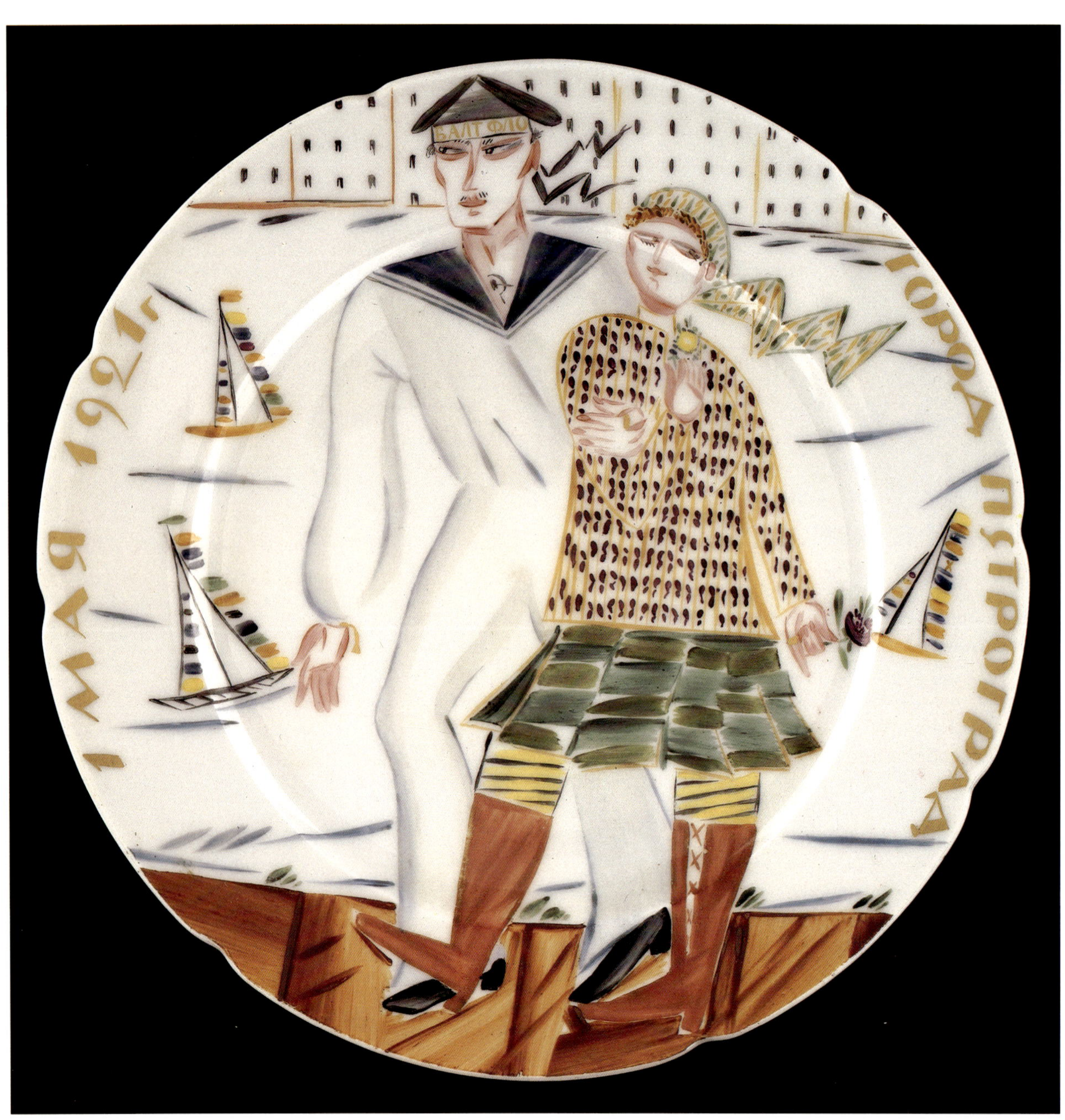

NO. 25
Aleksandra
Shchekotikhina-
Pototskaia
*Plate called "The Sailor
Takes a Walk,"* 1921

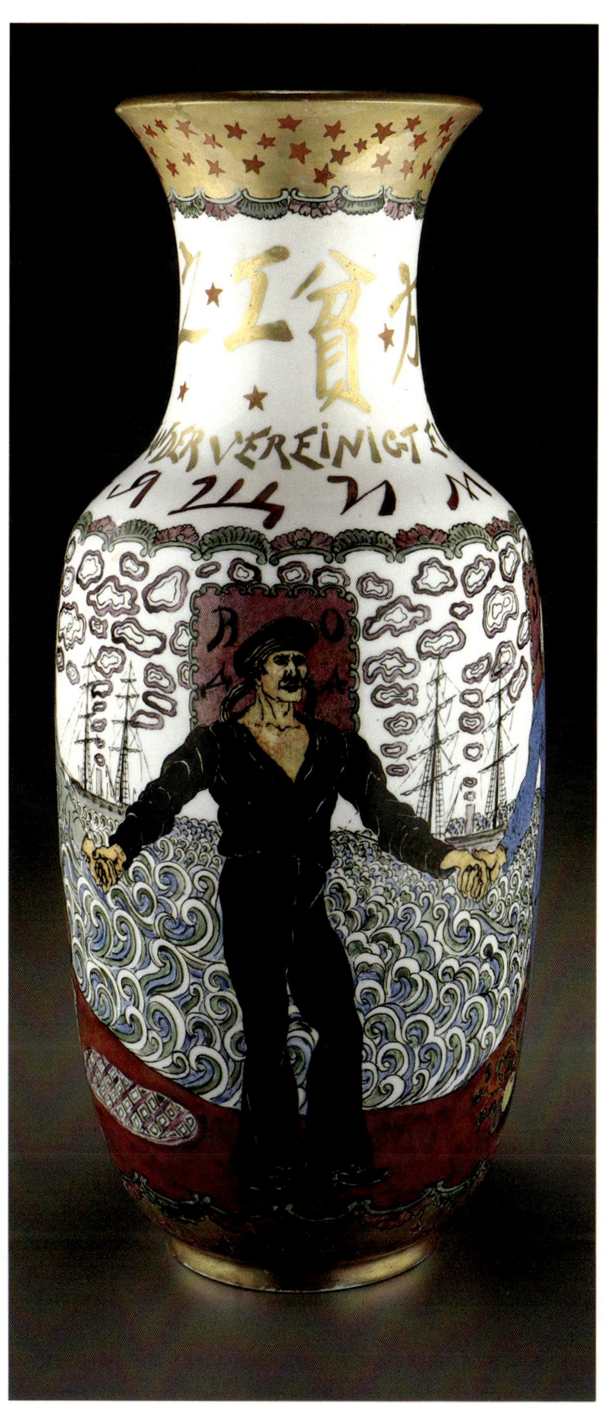
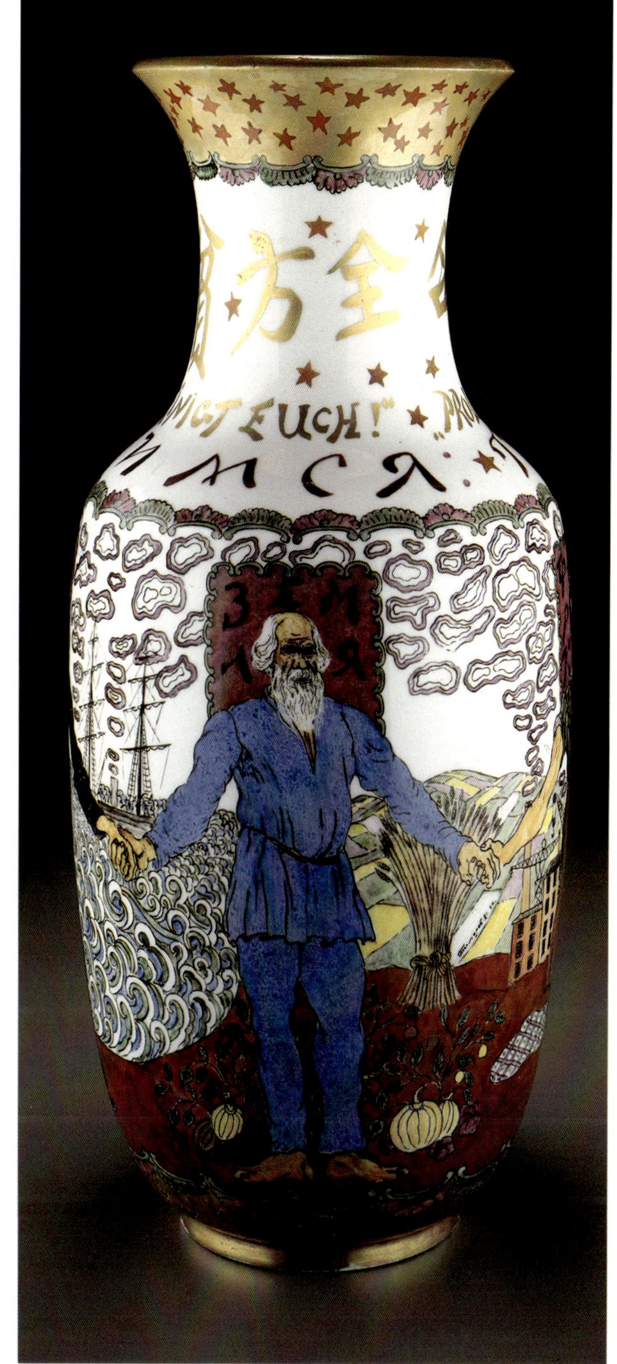

ernment to do mosaic designs for the tomb of King George I in 1914,[21] was acquainted with the fine points of royal practice: where in earlier examples the gilding modeled neoclassical motifs, carrying imperial associations since Roman times, now the gilding depicts agrarian and industrial tools, symbols of the "kingdom of the worker." The adroit burnishing, which subtly replicates such details as the wood grain in the architect's triangle, forcefully equates the empire and the workers' state—that is, that the tools of labor are to the worker what pomp and circumstance were to the tsar. The designer has also borrowed the eighteenth-century stylization of letters as ropes of flowers, seen in such earlier examples as the service of Count Il'ia Andreevich Bezborodko, c. 1784, for the initials of the Russian Republic.[22] Finally, the bold red star balances these decorative devices, clearly signaling how to read Adamovich's intentions in borrowing techniques. The ability to burnish with such facility and to letter with such delicacy obviously belongs to workers trained before the Revolution. The designer has found a way to save these luxury techniques and put them to use, just as the high quality blanks themselves were preserved and provided such a perfect ground for the

post-Revolutionary painters. Other plates in the Tuber collection indicate that burnishing in gold and silver (see cat. no. 35) and flower designs (see cat. nos. 14, 22) were techniques used repeatedly in the factory.

Finally there are functions of the porcelain that straddle the boundary of 1917. It is curious but true that though Soviet propaganda porcelains were conceived for the proletariat, they were not consumed by them. Slogans like "The kingdom of the workers and peasants will never end" (see cat. no. 10) addressed the proletariat, and themes from famine to literacy raised urgent issues facing the entire populace. And yet the hand-painted ceramics were produced in too small a number to reach many people, or to be affordable by any but the privileged or foreign visitors. Furthermore, the many avant-garde and abstract designs did not appeal to the majority of the public, accustomed to more traditional art forms. As in the late nineteenth century, one important role of porcelain continued to be that of revenue-producing export, particularly by the time of the 1925 International Exposition of Decorative and Industrial Arts, Paris, where a large display was mounted in the Soviet pavilion. Since the wares were increasingly intended for those outside the borders, it

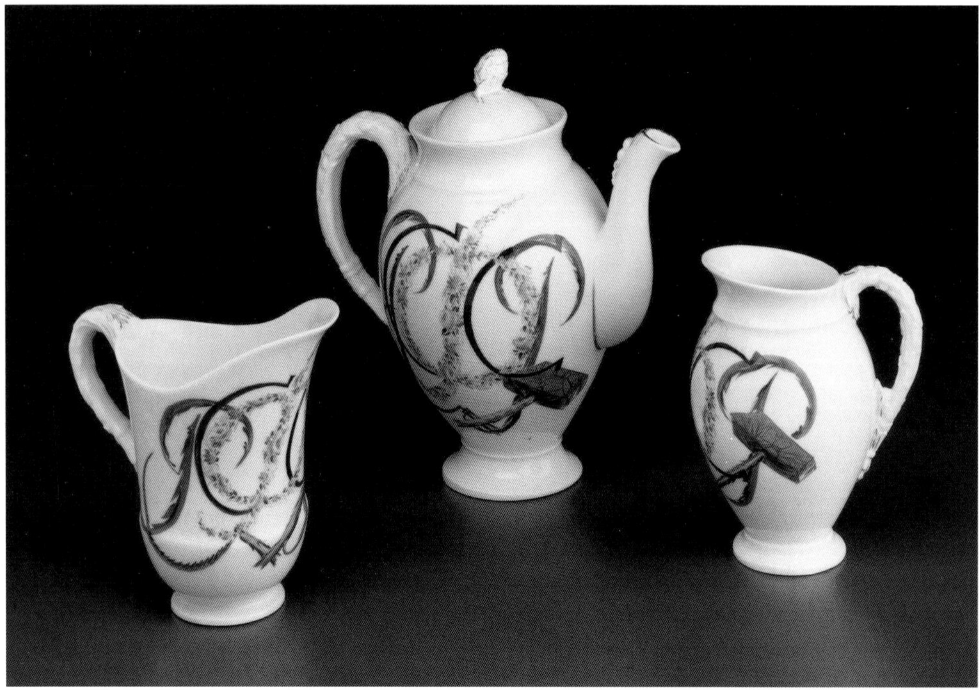

NO. 14
Sergei Chekhonin
Milk jug, teapot, hot-water jug, 1934

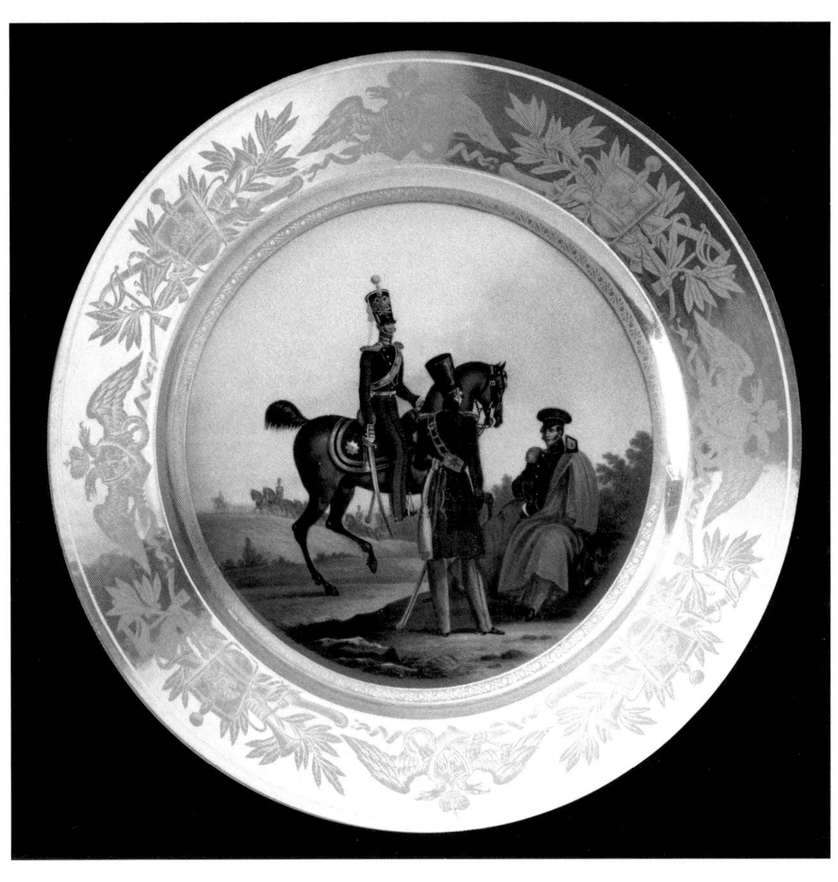

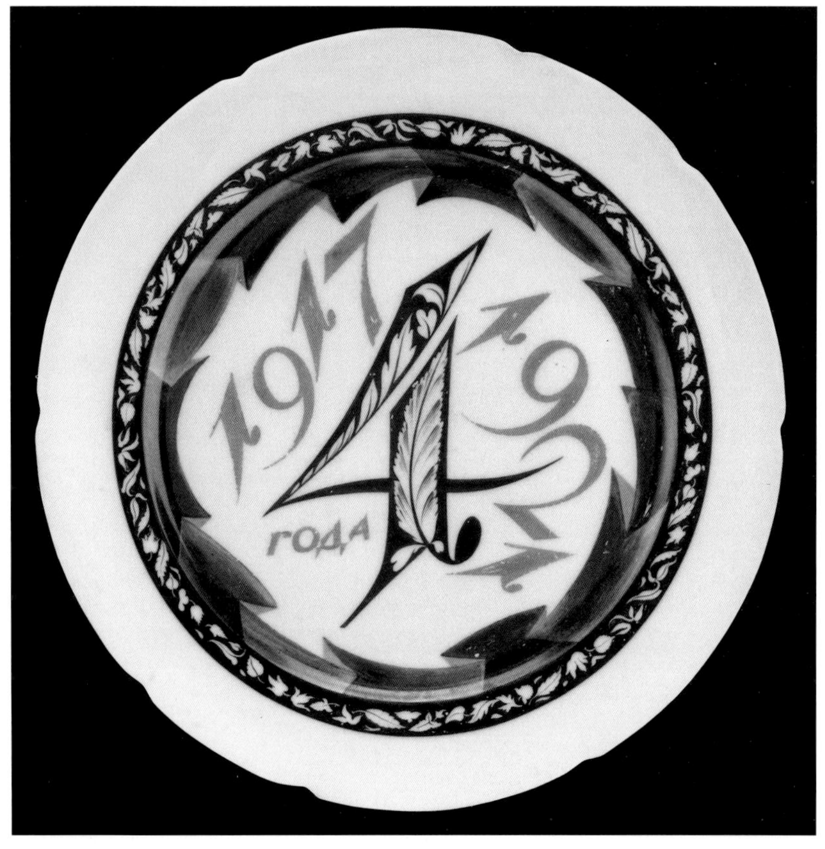

FIGURE 6

Imperial Porcelain Factory, painted by V. Stoletov, *plate depicting soldiers from the Horse Guards Regiment*, porcelain, c. 1831. Collection of Raymond F. Piper (photo by Dennis Schwartz).

NO. 13

Sergei Chekhonin

Plate, 1921

is not surprising that principal patrons of the State Porcelain Factory were ambassadors. Like the nobility in previous centuries, embassies commissioned services. Chekhonin designed a service for forty-eight based on Aleksandr Pushkin's 1820 epic poem *Ruslan and Liudmila* for the Soviet embassy in Berlin in 1925.[23]

Another primary reason for the creation of porcelain remained: commemorating anniversaries and honoring events. Since the eighteenth century, the Gardner Factory's order services had been made to celebrate the feast days of the patron saints of each order, and the tsars had ordered cups to commemorate their coronations and to be given away as mementos. The Soviet tradition of celebrating events by commissioning ceramics is particularly well represented in the Tuber collection. The anniversary of the Revolution,

October 25 (celebrated, according to the Gregorian calendar, on November 7), was noted every year with designs from the State Porcelain Factory (see cat. nos. 34, 41). The Congress of the Soviets (see cat. no. 21) and May Day, the international holiday of working people, were other dates marked by the plates.

When its workers took over the Imperial Porcelain Factory in 1918, they instituted changes that achieved a new dynamic for porcelain decoration. The rigorous demands of the social order and the climate of experimentation in the arts, together with the invitation to graphic artists, painters, and others from outside the field of ceramics to design for porcelain, led to a series of startlingly inventive plates. Designs were eclectic, quality was uneven, and production limit-

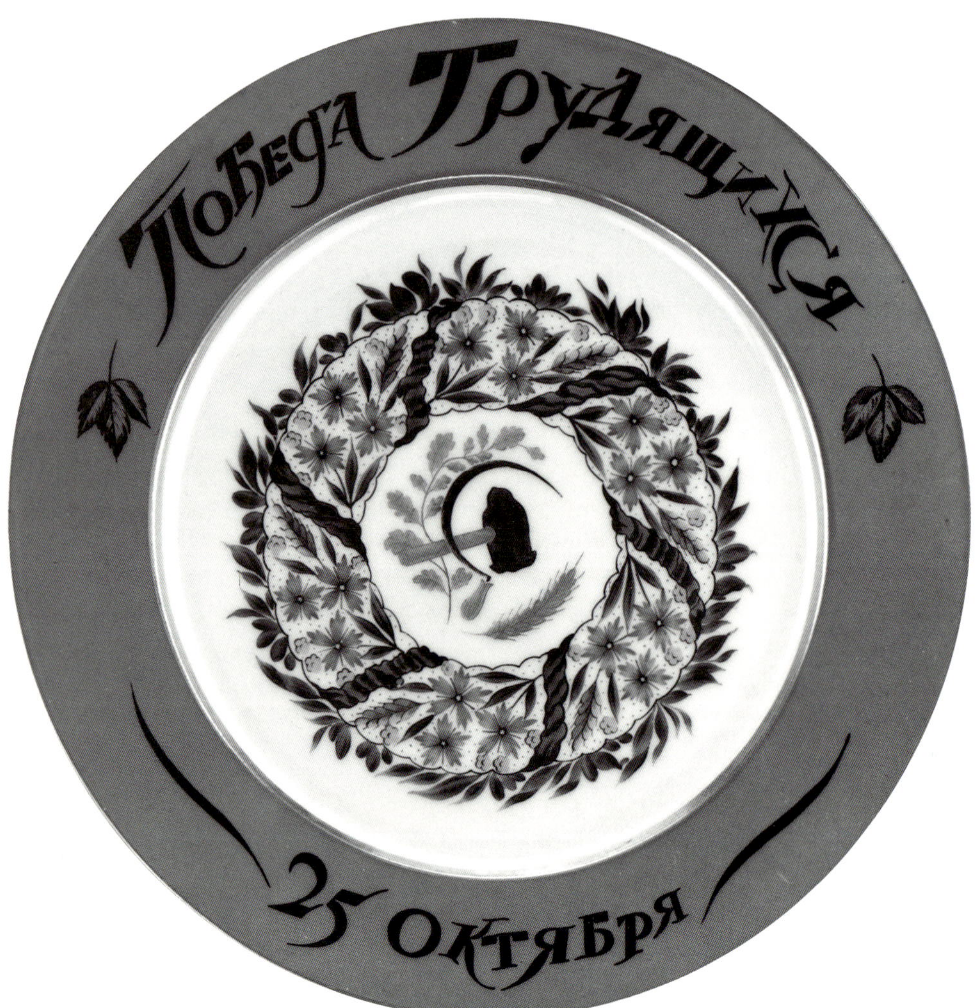

NO. 38

Rudol'f Vil'de

Plate, 1922

ed. But the symbolic value for the Revolution and the creative qualities of this revitalized art form were extraordinarily high. The State Porcelain Factory's dependence on earlier tradition should not be overemphasized; its innovations in design are strikingly evident. Yet it takes nothing away from these achievements to point out what the new owed to the old. It only adds to the rich complexity and irony of Soviet ceramics that they often depended on previous examples. Bent over the blanks in the factory, the painters must have shaken with excitement at the shattering recent experience they were conveying in their work. The act of painting these delicate objects seemed to promise the "radiant future" of the Revolution. Still, the beauty of the porcelain blanks, the fragile survivors of two centuries of Russian production, was the basis of their work, and in turning to these pure white surfaces, the painters paid homage to a lost era.

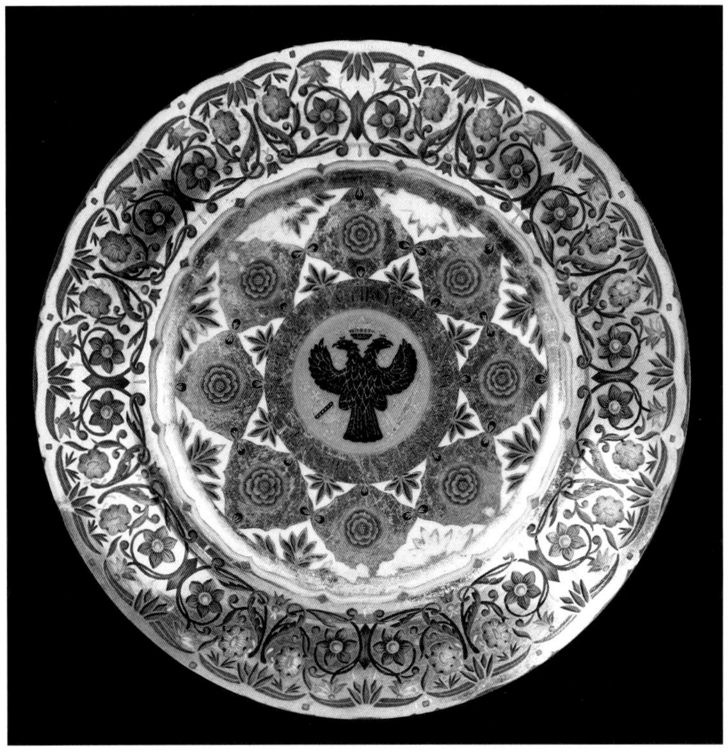

NOTES

1. See *Faiences et objets Revolutionnaires: P. M. Sestié Collection*, exh. cat. Conservatoire François Joseph Gossec, Gagny (1989). See also Edith Manroni, *Les faiences Revolutionnaires* (Paris, 1989).

2. See David Eliot, "Art into Production," in *Art into Production: Soviet Textiles, Fashion and Ceramics, 1917–1935*, exh. cat. Oxford Museum of Modern Art (1984), p. 6.

3. Nina V. Vernova, "Services from the Russian Imperial Palaces," in *An Imperial Fascination: Porcelain*, exh. cat. A la Viéille Russie, New York (1991), p. 17.

4. See Baron N. B. von Wolf, *Imperatorskii farforovyi zavod 1744–1904* (Saint Petersburg, 1906), p. 329 (summary in French). See also L. Nikiforova, *Russkii farvor v Ermitazhe/Russian Porcelain in the Hermitage* (Leningrad, 1973), p. 6; and Kathryn B. Hiesinger, "Soup Plate for the Private Service of Empress Elizabeth of Russia, c. 1756," *Philadelphia Museum Bulletin* 80, nos. 343–44 (Summer/Fall 1984), pp. 16–17.

5. Richard Hare, "Porcelain of the Russian Empire," *Connoisseur* 142, no. 572 (Nov. 1958), p. 98.

6. Richard Hare, *The Art and Artists of the Russian Empire* (London, 1965), p. 145.

7. Hare (note 5), p. 100, points out that the Arabesque Service "served an ulterior purpose by illustrating Russian naval victories, the Crimea brought under the protection of Russia, etc."

8. See G. Bernard Hughes, "An English Potter's Triumph in Imperial Russia," *Country Life* 133 (Feb. 28, 1963), pp. 408–10.

9. For a discussion of the orders, see Valentina M. Nikitina, "The Tsar's Highest Favor: Russian Orders and Medals," in *Moscow Treasures and Traditions*, exh. cat. Smithsonian Institution Traveling Exhibition Service, Washington, D.C. (1990), pp. 132–41. See also A. W. Hazelton, *The Russian Imperial Orders* (New York, 1932).

10. For examples of the Order Services, see *An Imperial Fascination* (note 3), cat. nos. 319–34.

11. For examples of the Gur'ev Service, see *An Imperial Fascination* (note 3), cat. nos. 50–77.

12. For discussions of Rachette's work, see G. Lukomsky, *Russisches Porzellan* (Berlin, 1924), p. 11; and Hare (note 5), p. 100.

13. See Katrina V. H. Taylor, "Hallmarks of Perfection: Porcelain of the Moscow Region," in *Moscow Treasures and Traditions* (note 9), p. 171.

14. For example, see *An Imperial Fascination* (note 3), cat. no. 117.

15. See *An Imperial Fascination* (note 3), cat. nos. 184–85.

16. See Eugenia Kirichenko, *Russian Design and the Fine Arts, 1750–1917* (New York, 1991), pp. 78–86.

See also Anne Odom, "Feodor Solntsev, the Kremlin Service, and the Origins of the Russian Style," *Hillwood Studies,* no. 1 (Fall 1991), pp. 1–4.

17. See Katrina V. H. Taylor, *Russian Art at Hillwood* (Washington, D.C., 1988), p. 78, fig. 116. See also Kirichenko (note 16), pp. 135ff.

18. An excellent discussion of this subject is found in Mariana Bubcikova, "Il rapporto fra i modelli della porcellana di propaganda e la tradizione artistica," in *La Rivoluzione in salotto: Porcellane sovietiche, 1917–1930,* exh. cat. Comune di Venezia (Milan, 1988), pp. 13–19.

19. Ibid., figs. 25–26.

20. See Taylor (note 17), fig. 99.

21. *Art into Production* (note 2), p. 133.

22. See *An Imperial Fascination* (note 3), cat. no. 336.

23. V. Filatov, "Soviet Porcelain," trans. in *Art into Production* (note 2), p. 15.

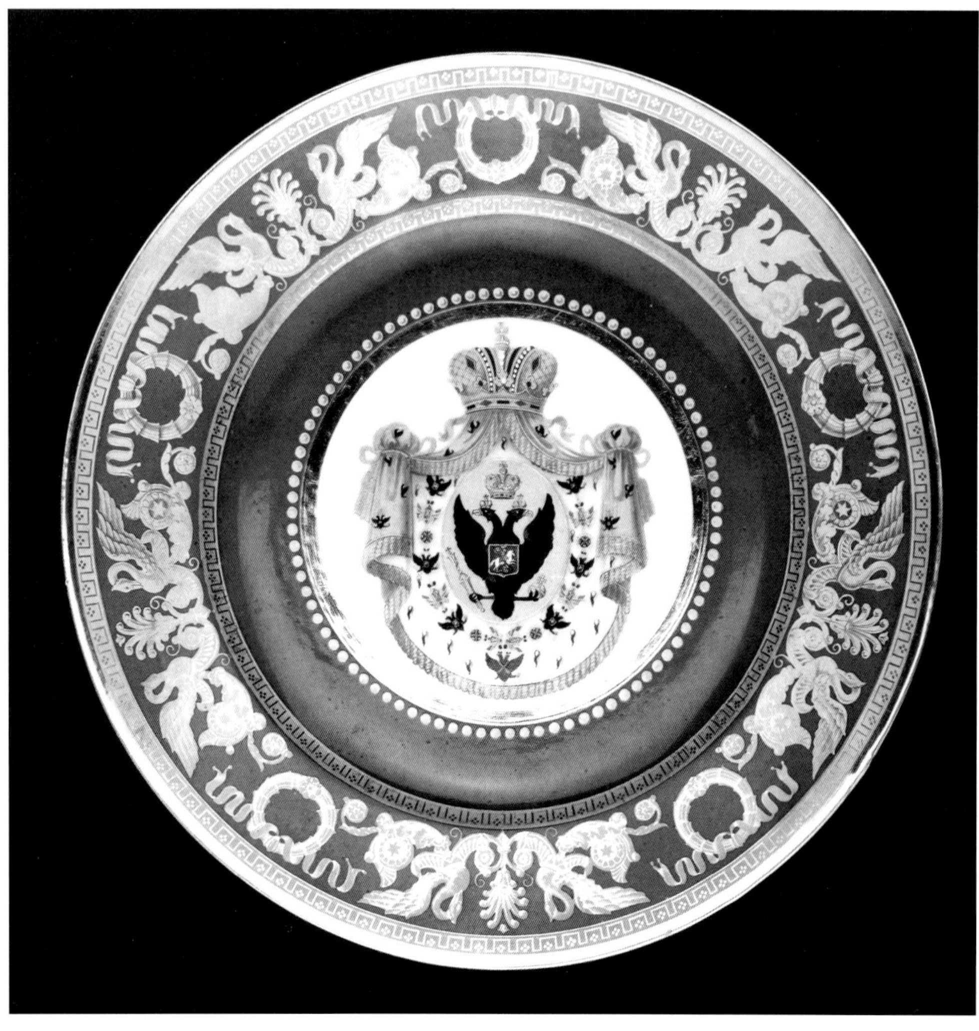

FIGURE 8

Imperial Porcelain Factory, *plate, probably from the Coronation Service of Alexander II,* porcelain, c. 1855/56. The Art Institute of Chicago, gift of John Wentworth (1942.40).

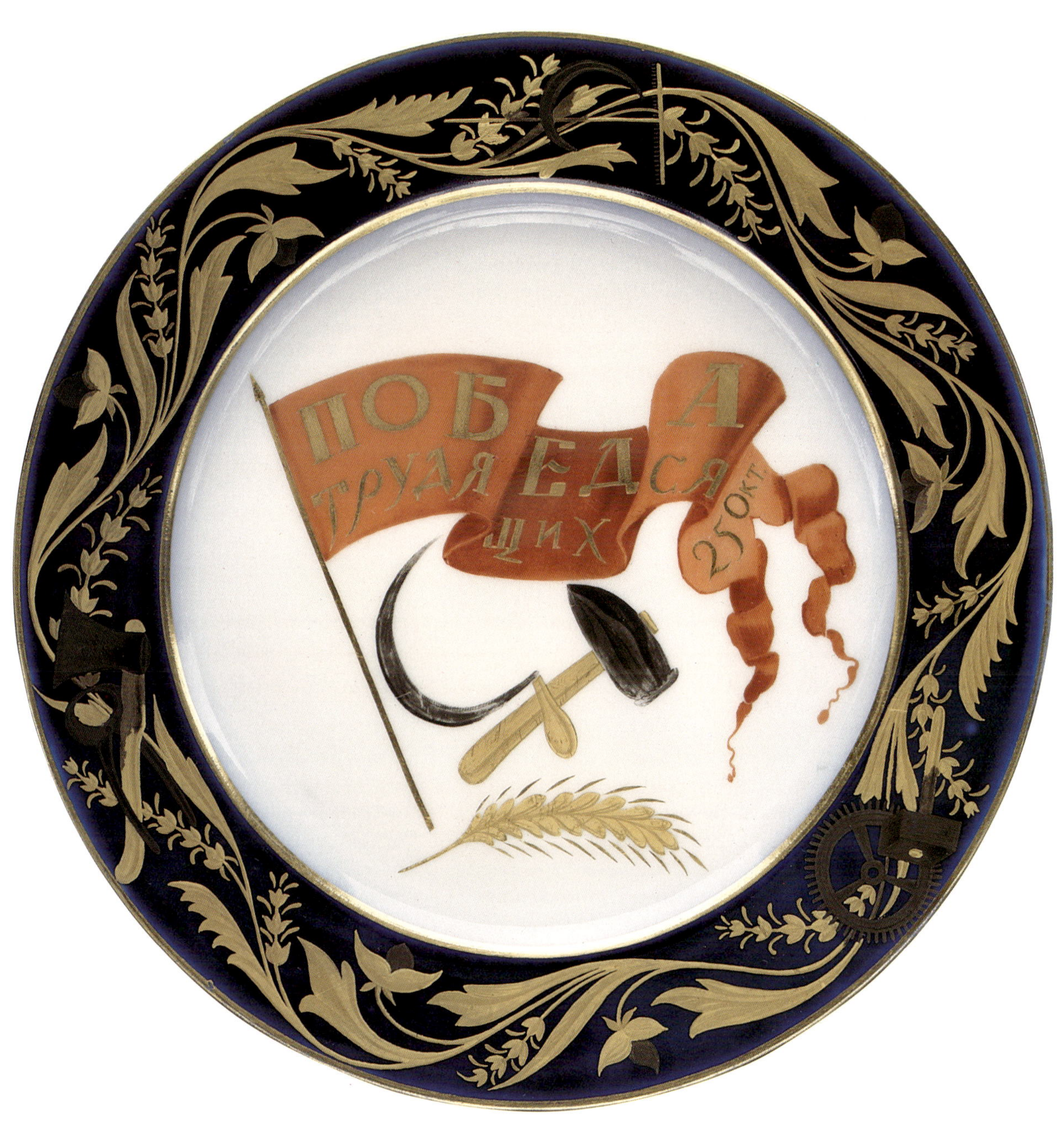

NO. 35
Rudol'f Vil'de
Plate, 1921

Tempest in a Teacup: Soviet Porcelain and the October Revolution

JOHN E. BOWLT, *Professor of Slavic Languages and Literatures, University of Southern California*

The period of revolution and civil war in Russia (1917–22) was a time of economic chaos, material deprivation, and cultural disorientation. While we now appreciate the political and artistic fervor of those years, it is easy to forget just how dislocated Russian society was. Ravaged by the misfortunes of World War I, revolution, and mass emigration, the Russian populus experienced extreme hardships and deficits at all levels. It was a case of bare survival, not least for artists, and a principal reason why so many— leftist and rightist—responded to the call for politicized art forms (the Plan of Monumental Propaganda put forth by Lenin, agitational art, mass actions) was perhaps more a material than an ideological one.

How curious it is that the October Revolution, a political episode that forced an almost feudal empire into a modern socialist state and that upset the global balance of political and economic power, should now be remembered by a material legacy of extreme fragility and delicacy. Those artifacts of the Revolutionary period that express most vividly its metamorphoses are fragile plates, plaster-of-Paris statues, and books and posters printed on highly acidic paper. Born of turbulence and transformation, these items were eternal in their ideas, but ephemeral in their outward forms. They broke, cracked, and tore, and yet many endured the ravages of war, political machination, and the caprice of fashion. The fact that the forty-five exhibited pieces of early Soviet porcelain from the Tuber collection have survived is ample testimony to this paradox of history, as well as to the diligence and originality of the Russian creative spirit.[1] The majority of these plates, dishes, cups, and saucers were made within the space of just two or three years, by a single factory, the State Porcelain Factory in Petrograd. Indeed, we are surprised to learn that, in spite of the turmoil of revolution and civil war, the State Porcelain Factory continued to produce ceramic articles at a frenetic rate: over three million items of "technological porcelain" (such as insulators and optical components) between July 1918 and the fall of 1919,[2] and "several thousand" artistic pieces between 1917 and 1921,[3] while the Paint Shop alone produced seventeen thousand items in 1919 (see fig. 1).[4] According to the porcelain artist Elena Dan'ko, the factory sent the first crates of export porcelain abroad, to Riga, Lithuania, in the fall of 1920.[5]

The kind of art and design generated by the Revolution—political porcelain, monumental statuary, open-air spectacles, flying banners, and mass literature—actually disguised a dearth of solid, durable artistic creations during the first years of the new republic. The history of art and design then is as much the history of what was not produced as of what was: it was a time of elaborate theory and meager practice, of visionary projects for a utopian future, of models and prototypes that could never be manufactured. Moreover, not all artists were keen to offer their services to the Revolution. Although many were attracted by Lenin's Plan of Monumental Propaganda of April 1918 (whereby statues to the heroes of socialism were to be erected in the streets and squares) and the program of agitational, or agit-, art (redesigning and redecorating buildings with posters, banners, and billboards celebrating the Revolution), everyday reality did not seem to change much, as the critic Platon Kerzhentsev observed:

You go into a Soviet restaurant, or any institution, a railroad station, a club or a new theater. Do you see the hand of an artist? Everywhere is filth, disorder, and a lack of even the most primitive cultivation of beauty. For the most part they're just pigsties, repulsive sewers. Why aren't the

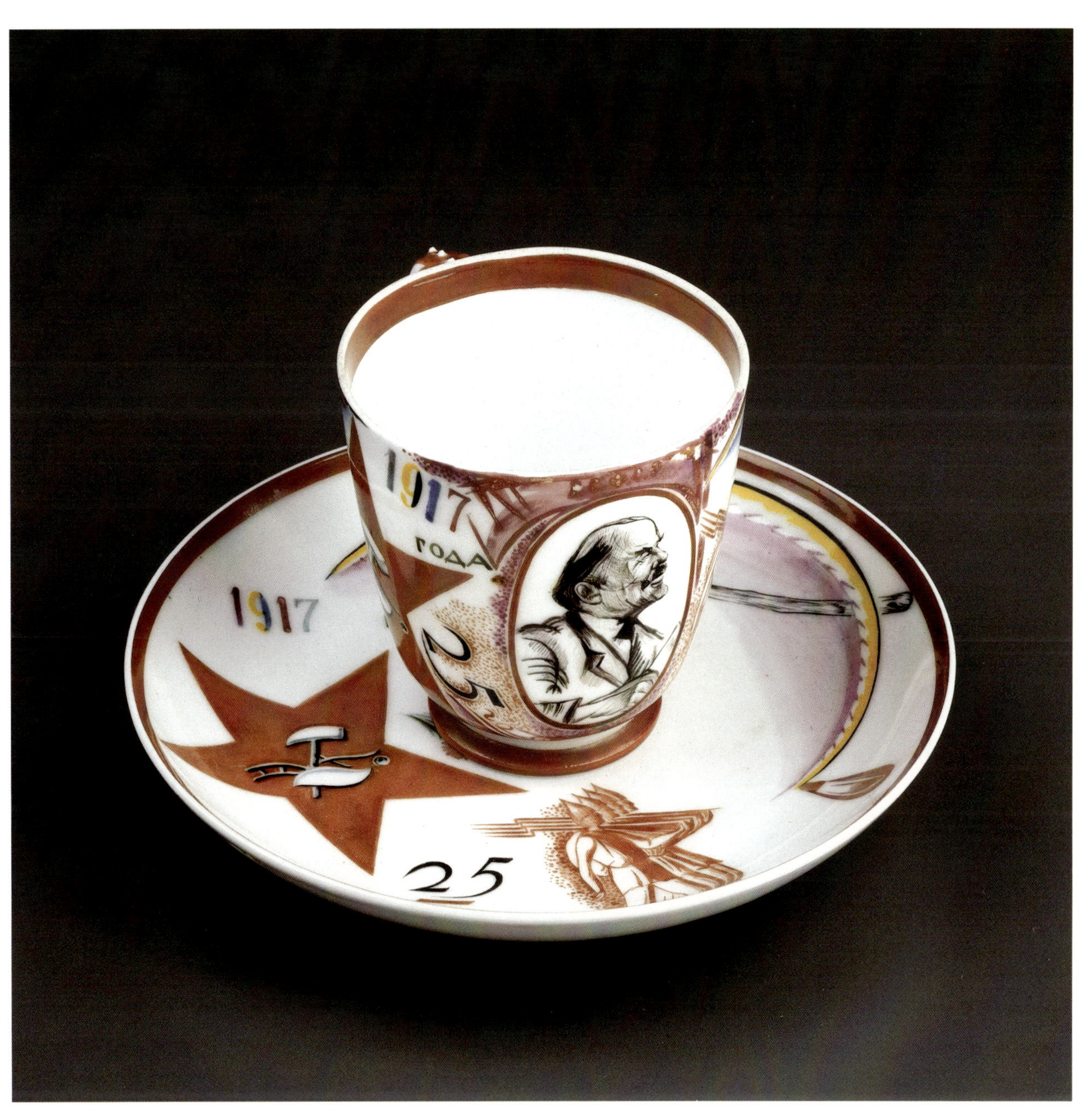

NO. 2
Mikhail Adamovich
*Cup and saucer
called "Lenin with
Red Star,"* 1921

31

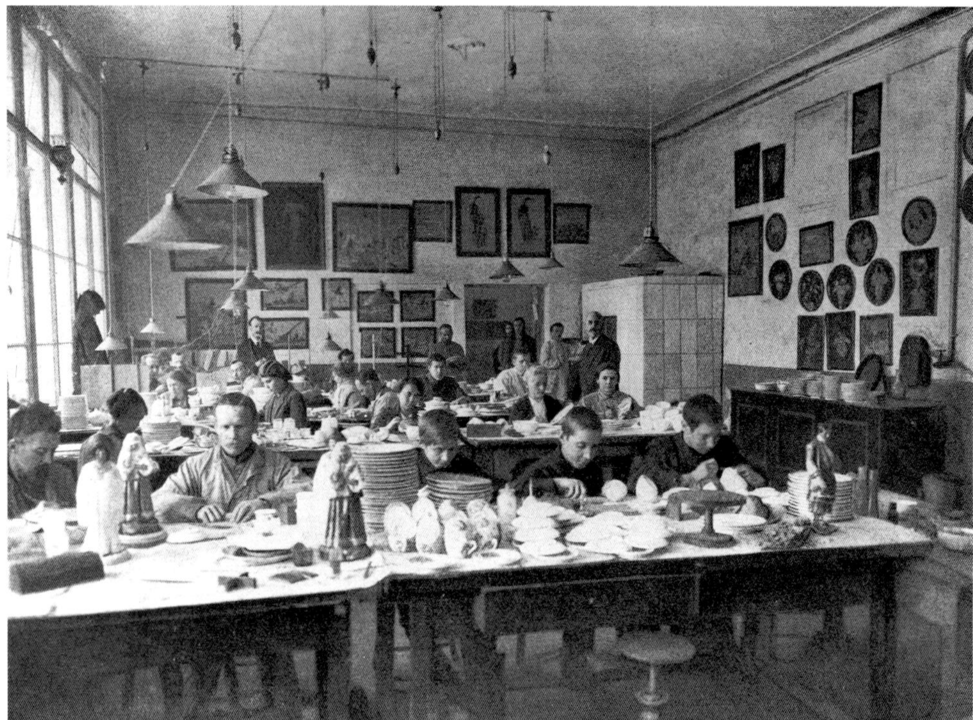

*artists indignant? Why don't they hang
their paintings, their posters, their pan-
neaux here? Why don't they paint the
walls of these rooms?*[6]

It is difficult to disperse the accumulat-
ed mythology surrounding the Revolution,
especially as far as the visual arts are concerned, and to assess the real predicament
of the artist then. But perhaps at least one
misconception can be questioned: the
notion of the October Revolution representing a clear dividing line between the old
culture and the new. The more we examine
the evolution of Russian culture during the
Modernist period, especially in the context
of design, the more we find that the apparent innovations of the early 1920s (e.g.,
Constructivism) derived immediately from
artistic concepts elaborated well before
1917. The Revolution certainly made this
generation of artists more aware of the
machine-made object, of industrial production, and of utilitarian design, but
their exposure to both cultural and technological experiment before the Revolution
was of profound importance to their stylistic maturity.

The Russian and Soviet ceramic industry is no exception. There was perhaps
more continuity here than change and, ultimately, it was this organic connection with
the imperial and bourgeois past—and its
"operatic treatment of revolutionary
images"[7]—that drew increasingly hostile
criticism from Marxist critics from the mid-
1920s onward. As the Constructivist Boris
Arvatov argued:

*The working class...will change its forms
of everyday life consciously, rationally,
and continuously....But this is only possible
if artists will stop decorating or depicting
life and start to build it.*[8]

Arvatov's complaints are understandable,
particularly with regard to agit-porcelain,
which was almost irrelevant to the masses
for whom, theoretically, it was created. Not
only was most of it manufactured in very
limited quantities, generally in editions
of two or three hundred,[9] but it was also
exported to the West for hard currency,
in spite of the "brisk trade" in the factory's
outlet on Nevskii Prospect.[10] Furthermore,
many of the designs were complex and
convoluted, requiring a sophisticated intel-
lect to decipher and appreciate the aesthetic and even the ideological messages
inscribed on the wares. The importance of

inscriptions made these items dependent on highly literate viewers in a country of massive illiteracy.

Many of the designers and painters of the agit-porcelain in this exhibition had been working in the Imperial and other porcelain factories well before the Revolution and often adapted their colors and forms to the exigencies of the new regime, while remaining loyal to their individual artistic styles (see fig. 2). Mariia Briantseva, Natal'ia Dan'ko, Zinaida Kobyletskaia, Vasilii Kuznetsov, and Rudol'f Vil'de had all been connected with the factory before the Revolution. Some of the most powerful of the agitational symbols are, in fact, paraphrases of the traditional iconic vocabulary, as Alison Hilton discusses in this volume. The torch-bearing rider on a winged horse in Alisa Golenkina's plate "The Red Genius" of 1922 (cat. no. 17) elicits immediate associations with the stereotypical Archangel Michael, while Vasilii Timorev's 1920 plate inscribed "He who is not with us is against us" (cat. no. 30) is a latter-day rendering of Saint George and the Dragon. Veniamin Belkin, Sergei Chekhonin, and Mikhail Dobuzhinskii, already known for their graphic mastery before the Revolution, extended their distinctive filigrees to early Soviet porcelain. Except for the ideological slogans, Chekhonin's floral patterns and Dobuzhinskii's *chinoiserie* would have been just at home on the pages of the neoclassical Saint Petersburg magazine *Apollon* (1909–17). Even the radical porcelain of Il'ia Chashnik, Kazimir Malevich, and Nikolai Suetin, inspired by Suprematism, often repeats geometric compositions that Malevich had painted in 1915–16, such as a 1923 plate carrying his image *Airplane Flying*. Above all, the State Porcelain Factory continued to produce commemorative artifacts in the same way that it had before the Revolution. Just as it had celebrated the Russian army, the nationalities of the empire, the tsar, and the church (issuing "one hundred thousand Easter eggs for the troops" during World War I),[11] so its agit-porcelain now fulfilled a similar function, except that "tsar" was replaced by "commune," and "Holy Russia" by "Russian Soviet Federal Socialist Republic."

The State Porcelain Factory was not, of course, a replica of the Imperial Porcelain Factory. Its administration was changed and its bureaucratic and fiscal structures were reformed. The able Evgenii Lansere (Lancéray), who had assumed directorship of the enterprise in 1913, left in the spring of 1917. The factory's staff was cut drastically, and, between the fall of 1917 and the spring of 1918, there were serious proposals to close the factory or to make it a purely industrial resource. Only through the offices of David Shterenberg, head of IZO (the Fine Arts Section of Anatolii Lunacharskii's Narkompros, the People's Commissariat of Enlightenment), was the factory saved from liquidation or demotion. Shterenberg had entrusted the Art Council for the Affairs of Industrial Design—composed of Ivan Bilibin, Chekhonin, Dobuzhinskii, Aleksandr Matveev, Nikolai Roerich (Rerikh), and Petr Vaulin—with the express assignment of examining the status of the factory, and their responsiveness and alacrity should be remembered with particular appreciation. Vaulin wrote to Lunacharskii in January 1918:

The Porcelain and the Glass Factories... cannot just be factory and industrial enterprises. They must be scientific and artistic centers. Their aim is to encourage the development of Russia's ceramic and glass industry, to seek and research new paths in production...to study and develop artistic form.[12]

Vaulin, a ceramicist who was appointed Commissar of the State Porcelain Factory in 1918 (despite protests from the rank and file), was a primary force.[13] Although his role at the factory and in the history of Russian ceramics in general has been neglected, his experience as a master ceramicist, original theorist, and astute businessman contributed a great deal to the practical innovations at the factory just after the Revolution. Vaulin, along with Aleksei Filippov (also an important Russian and then Soviet teacher, theorist, and critic of ceramics)[14] and Vladimir Frolov (an enamelist and tile specialist), had earned a national reputation as a pioneer in the development and application of glazed tiles and luster ware in the early 1900s. Vaulin was a disciple of Mikhail Vrubel', whose productions at Savva Mamontov's Ceramic Factory (founded in Abramtsevo in 1889 and then moved to Moscow in 1896) were among the most innovative artistic productions of the Symbolist era. Under Vaulin's supervision, the Moscow factory produced highly experimental pottery in the Art Nouveau style and received many advantageous commissions, such as the ceramic details for Moscow's Yaroslavl Station. Vrubel' himself conducted bold experiments in the actual manufacture of ceramics, especially with glazing process-es. The particular iridescence and sheen that he attained in works such as *Spes* (1899) and *Poetry* (c. 1900), and his choice of greens, purples, and carmines, left a deep imprint on an entire generation of Russian artists, such as the Murava ceramicists' community and the studios of

the Stieglitz and Stroganov schools of art and design. Vaulin, Frolov, and other leading exponents of Art Nouveau in Russia experienced the lasting effect of Vrubel's ceramic resolutions. The glazed tiles Vaulin produced for the facades of Saint Petersburg homes at his own Artistic Ceramic Manufactory in Kikerino, near Saint Petersburg, from 1906 onward would hardly have been possible without the discoveries of Vrubel'. Vaulin and his colleagues enriched this heritage by exploring further the possibilities of purely abstract design, investigating asymmetry, dissonance, and syncopation as cardinal artistic principles. With his inquiring mind, rich imagination, and untiring search for radical forms, Vaulin also appealed to the avant-garde artists of Saint Petersburg. The Futurist painter Nikolai Kul'bin even included some of Vaulin's works in his exhibitions, especially at "The Triangle" of 1910 in Saint Petersburg.

It is important to remember that Chekhonin, Aleksandr Matveev, and other leading painters and designers of the 1900s apprenticed under Vaulin in Moscow or Kikerino, established a recognizable school of modern Russian ceramics, and contributed directly or indirectly to the development of both the Imperial and the State Porcelain Factory. Vaulin's position there in the early Soviet period emphasizes, therefore, the perpetuation, rather than the abolition, of certain key principles—innovative design, individual interpretation, and also professional universality, in the sense that the porcelain designer was expected to know the entire process of manufacture, from the clay model to the painting and firing. Chekhonin, who began to work with porcelain in 1913 and who was appointed head of the Artistic Section of the State Porcelain Factory in 1917, was a keen supporter of these principles. Unlike some of the painters who submitted designs to the factory between 1919 and 1921, he was convinced that "porcelain is not painting" and that "the designs received from artists who themselves are not working at the Factory create many, many problems."[15]

As far as the agit-porcelain is concerned, Chekhonin must have been irritat-

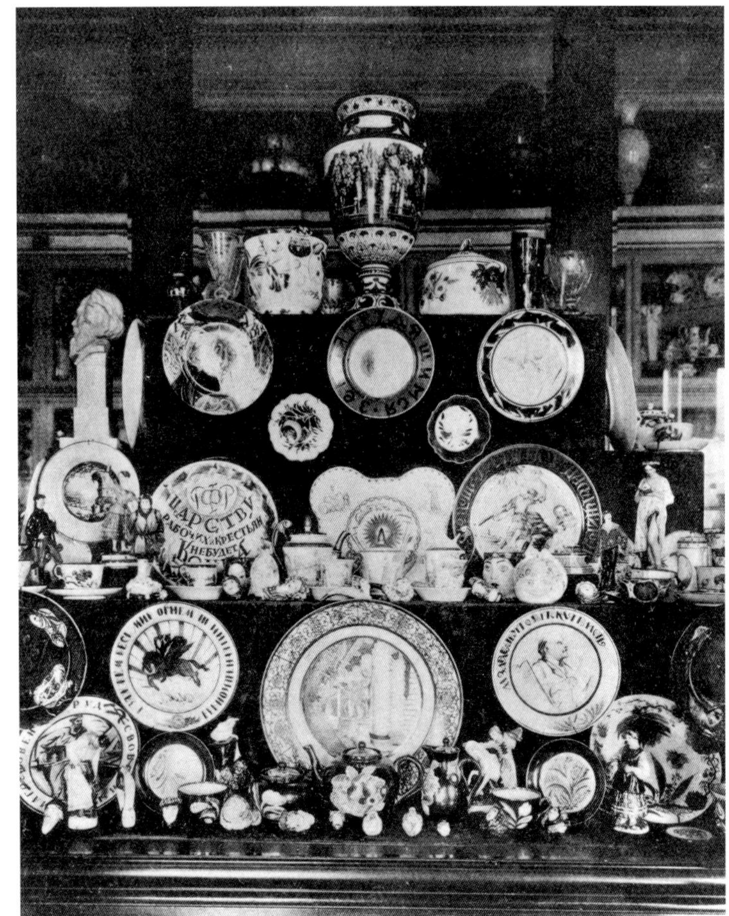

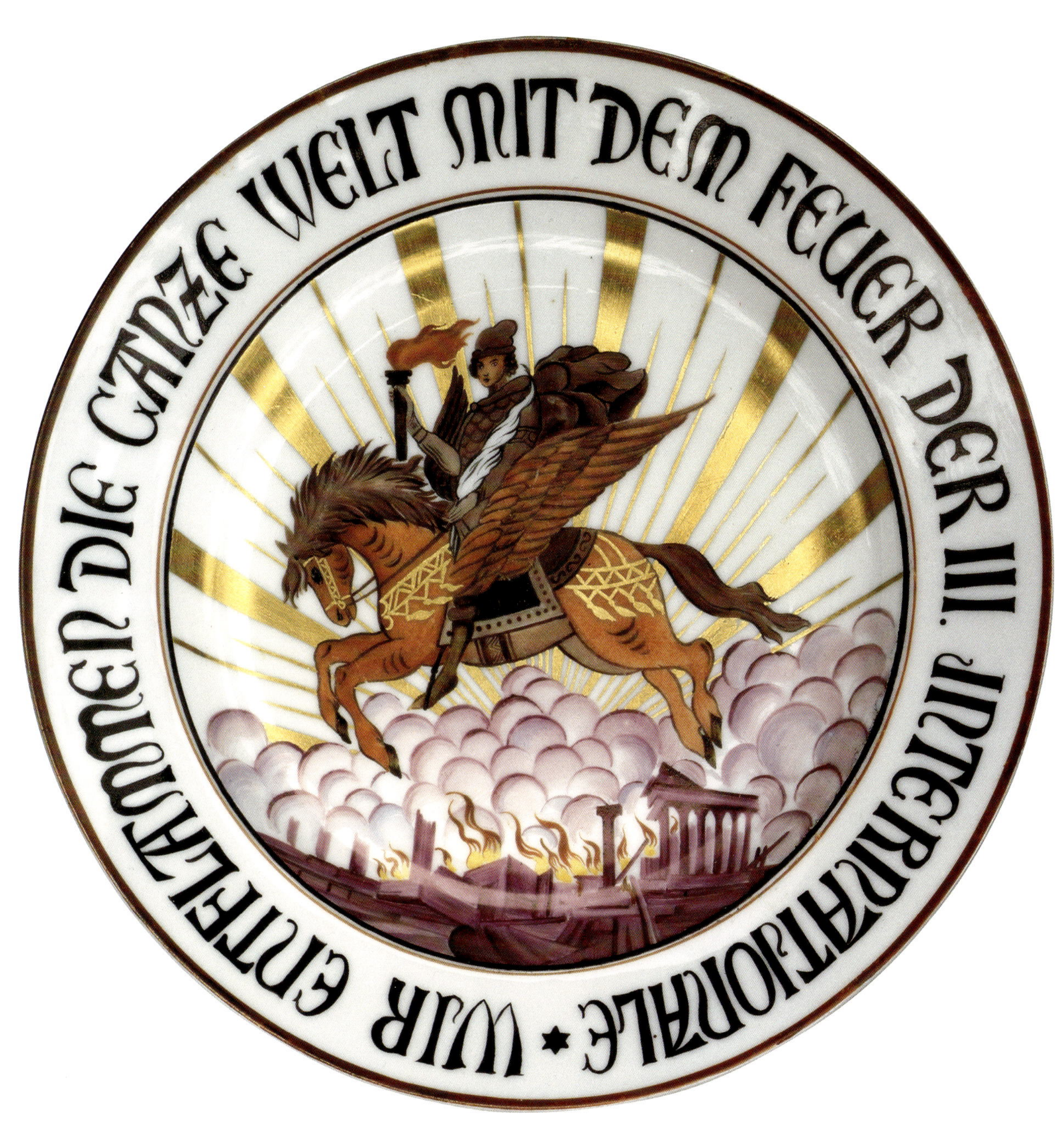
DIE GANZE WELT MIT DEM FEUER DER III. INTERNATIONALE WIR ENTFLAMMEN

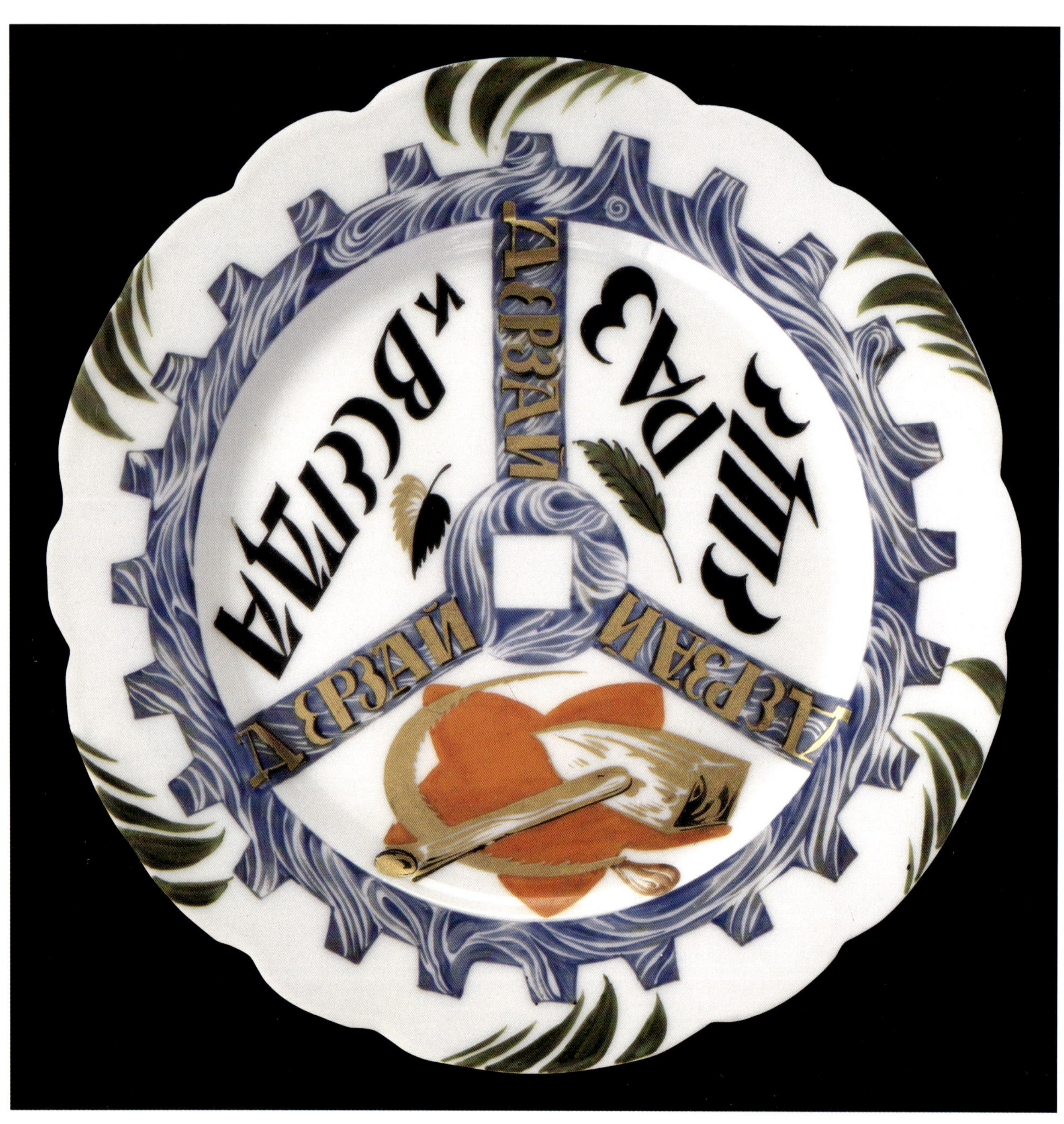

NO. 33
Rudol'f Vil'de
Plate, 1921

ed by the artistic incongruities produced by some of his colleagues, although he himself was not entirely innocent. Not all the maxims inscribed on agit-porcelain were lucid or even appropriate—"Be brave again and always" (see cat. no. 33), for example, is rather ambiguous. The critic Erik Gollerbakh made this clear in his article "Siuzhety i kharakter zhivopisi po farforu" (Themes and character of porcelain painting) of 1924, in which he chided Kobyletskaia for some of her fanciful compositions and ingenuous slogans.[16] "There's nothing easier than painting porcelain," wrote one ceramics teacher rashly in 1908,[17] and the superabundance of highly decorated kitsch in early twentieth-century Russian porcelain demonstrates the accuracy of this statement, as well as the dangers of indiscriminate taste and of form that is poorly coordinated with function.

These problems aside, the distinguishing features of the State Porcelain Factory during its first years are the interpretation of the ceramic artifact as a vehicle of ideological propaganda and the concentration on the verbal message. Here again, this is a conventional rather than an innovative approach, for the history of Russian culture is, surely, one of a didactic, utilitarian, or "applied" art, whether we think of icons or realist novels, Wassily Kandinsky's theosophical painting or Petr Tchaikovsky's program music, or the rich tradition of nineteenth-century Russian porcelain inscribed with moral aphorisms, proverbs, and thematic explanations. This narrative or literary emphasis might relate to the dictatorial gesture, in that every word of the emperor or the high priest was a command to be implemented fully and unquestioningly. The inscriptions on agit-porcelain and posters share something of this autocratic enunciation, whereby the word *is* the deed, for they are so loud and so abrasive to the porcelain or paper surfaces that they seem already to be implementations rather than mere exhortations. It is a peculiar manipulation of words that later, in Stalin's Russia, caused the desired physical result to be replaced by the text, so that the White Sea Canal was considered "open" long before it was opened, and tourists were urged to visit the Palace of the Soviets in Moscow even though it was never built. Agit-plates with imperatives such as "Long live the Eighth Congress of the Soviets" on a plate by Elizaveta Rozendorf (cat. no. 21) and "Long live the Third International" on an Adamovich plate (cat. no. 1) maintained this traditional Russian attitude toward the word as both sacrosanct and active.

"In the beginning was the word"—this applies directly to the dawn of the secular Soviet state, which in the space of just twelve months issued over two hundred decrees and resolutions concerned with matters of art.[18] The captions, maxims, and slogans that we read in the propaganda of that time remind us constantly of the Bible and other ecclesiastical literature. "The kingdom of the workers and peasants will never end," proclaim two dishes in the Tuber Collection (cat. nos. 10, 11), echoing the Old Testament's "And His kingdom will have no end" or the familiar "Thine is the kingdom, and the power, and the glory, for ever" from the Lord's Prayer (Matt. 6:13). The famous "He who does not work, does not eat," inscribed on a 1922 plate by Mikhail Adamovich (cat. no. 4), para-

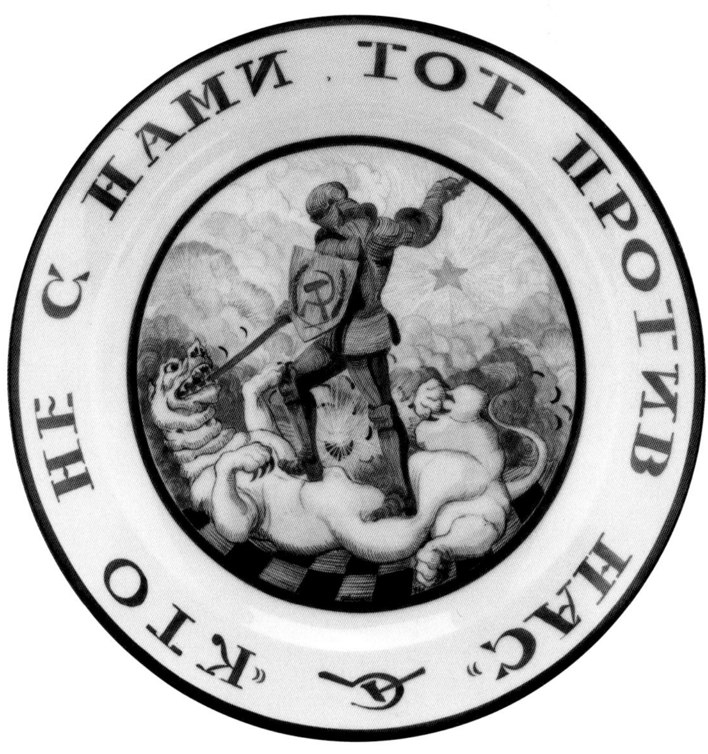

phrases Saint Paul, "If any would not work, neither should he eat" (2 Thess. 3:10). Belkin's plate inscribed "Blessed is free labor" (cat. no. 8) also relies on a religious ideal.

Many of the aphorisms that appear in agit-porcelain are from the list of slogans that Lenin ratified in connection with his Plan of Monumental Propaganda. According to his decree of April 1918:

[The Soviet of People's Commissars] is entrusted with mobilizing artistic forces and organizing an extensive competition for producing projects of monuments intended to commemorate the great days of the Russian Socialist Revolution....The same committee is also entrusted with urgently preparing the decoration of the city by May 1 and with replacing inscriptions, emblems, street names, coats of arms and so forth by new ones reflecting the ideas and feelings of the working class of revolutionary Russia.[19]

In accordance with this resolution, Narkompros, the People's Commissariat of Enlightenment, commissioned sculptors to design monuments to the luminaries

of social and political history for the streets and squares of the new Russia. Lunacharskii formed a committee composed of Valerii Briusov, Vladimir Friche, and Mikhail Pokrovskii to collect and edit aphorisms that could accompany this monumental propaganda. By September 1918, the committee had selected twenty-eight sayings attributed to Mikhail Bakunin, Nikolai Chernyshevskii, Confucius, Georges Danton, Fedor Dostoevsky, Ferdinand Lassalle, Karl Marx, Sir Thomas More, Ovid, Dmitrii Pisarev, John Ruskin, Max Stirner, Leo Tolstoi, and the Bible. Among them were statements that have become bywords of revolution, although the sources may have been forgotten: Stirner's "He who is not with us is against us" was used by Timorev on a plate of 1920 (cat. no. 30); "The mind cannot tolerate slavery," on an unattributed plate of 1922 (cat. no. 42), is from Pisarev, not from Grigorii Zinov'ev, as his silhouette there might lead us to believe; and the popular "The spirit of destruction is at the same time a creative one" is from the famed anarchist Bakunin.[20] Other aphorisms were simple appeals such as "Long live the power of the Soviets," used by Kobyletskaia in 1921 (cat. no. 18), or "Long Live the Red Army," used by Adamovich in 1923 (cat. no. 6). Others were contractions and acronyms such as R.S.F.S.R. (Russian Soviet Federal Socialist Republic), which many porcelain artists incorporated into their designs. Many of the thematic concepts presented on plates, such as literacy (see cat. no. 32), also relate directly to the priorities of Lenin's domestic program.

Given this strong orientation toward text, utterance, and command in Russian culture, and specifically in agit-porcelain, it should not come as a surprise to learn that a number of the key designers at the State Porcelain Factory, including Chekhonin, were also book illustrators. The critic Boris Emme even noted in his 1950 study of Russian porcelain that Chekhonin, "essentially a graphic artist of the book, created many items in porcelain, but in principle they differed little from his stylized graphic works."[21] Chekhonin, Dobuzhinskii, Mariia Ivashinskaia, Evgenii Narbut, and

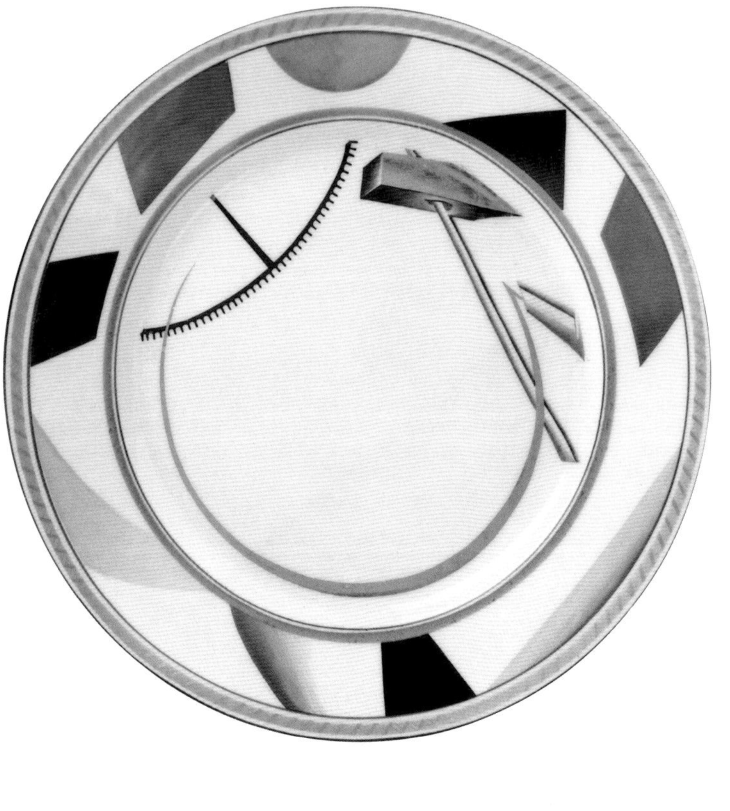

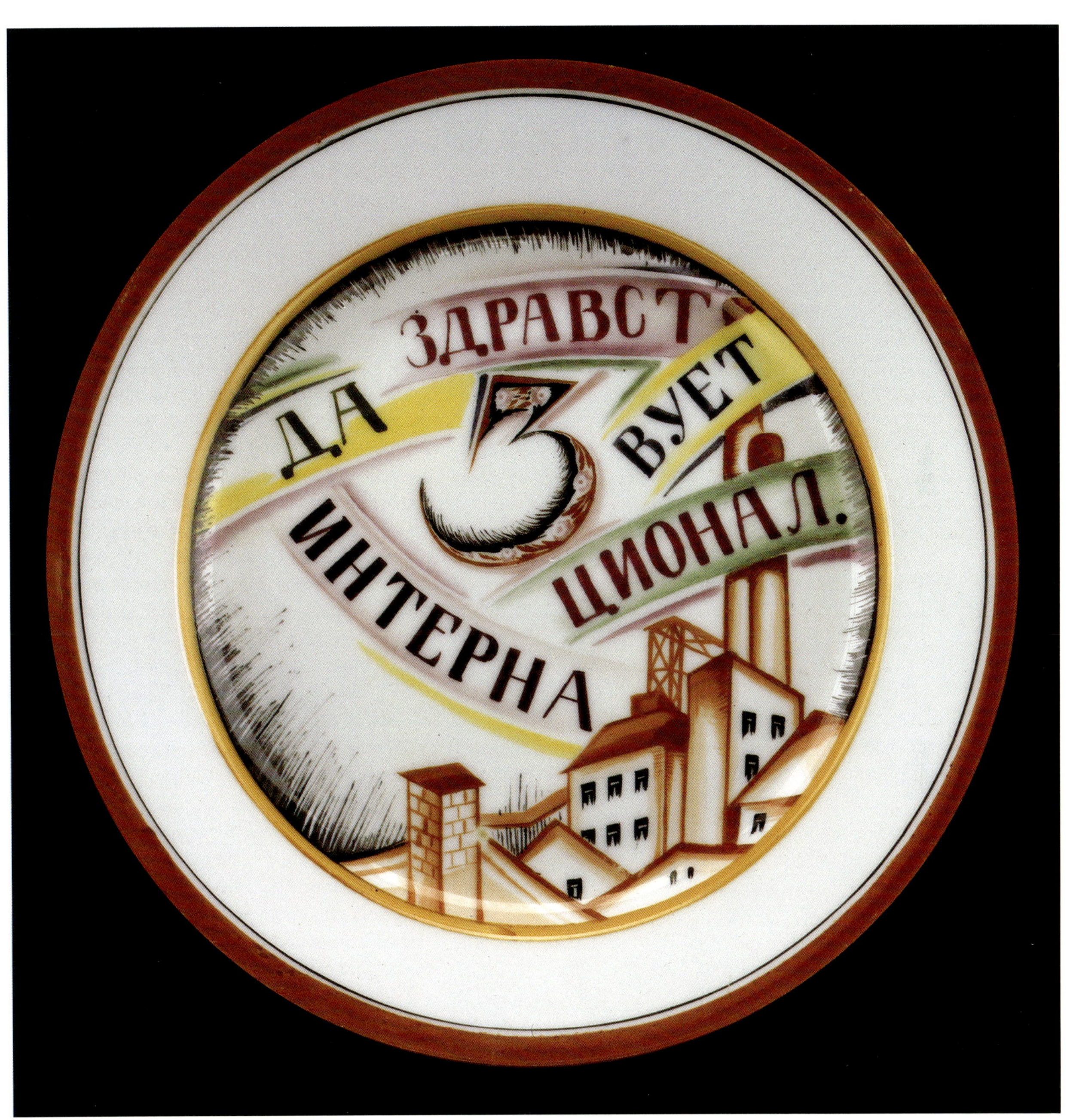

NO. 1

Mikhail Adamovich

Plate, 1921

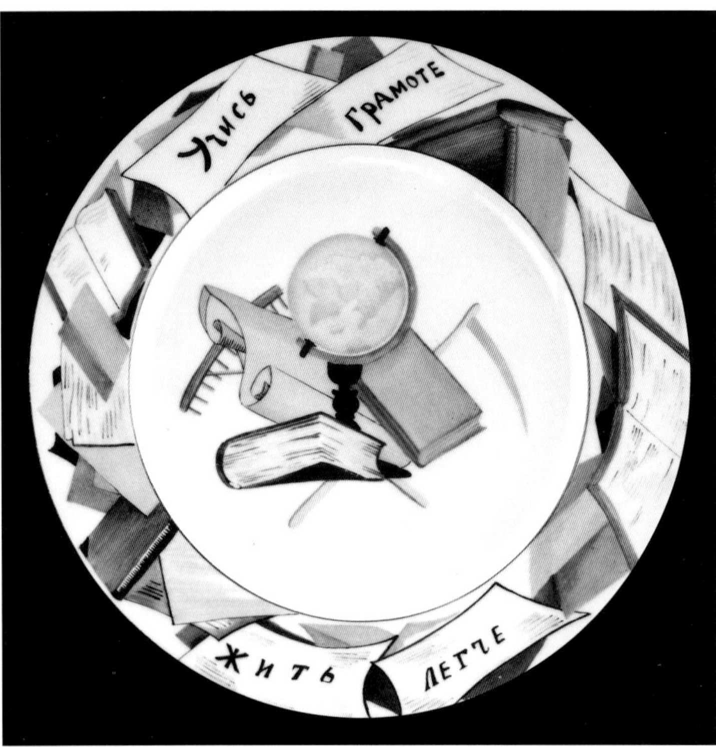

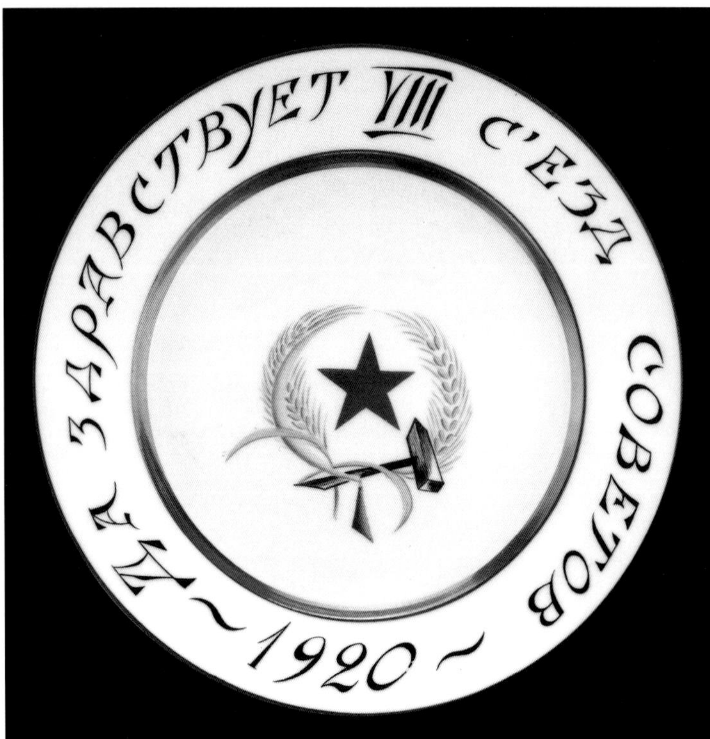

Top	Bottom
NO. 32	**NO. 21**
Attributed to	Elizaveta Berngardovna
Elizaveta Berngardovna	Rozendorf
Rozendorf	or Rudol'f Vil'de
Plate, 1920	*Plate*, 1920

Aleksandra Shchekotikhina-Pototskaia had all trained as studio artists before the Revolution and had already achieved reputations as book or stage designers. Indeed, some of the motifs that we encounter on the cups, saucers, and plates of around 1920 are borrowed from the fairy stories, poetry collections, and almanacs that they or their colleagues illustrated. Chekhonin actually transferred vignettes that he had made for *Apollon* in the early 1910s to his porcelain in the early 1920s (see figs. 3–4).[22]

As Gollerbakh asserted in his 1924 study, graphic finesse, decorative sensibility, and illustrative function guaranteed the high quality of porcelain just after the Revolution. In this sense, the State Porcelain Factory can be regarded as the last stronghold of the ideals of the *Apollon* and *Mir iskusstva* (World of Art) artists who had contributed so much to the efflorescence of the graphic and applied arts during the Silver Age, the turn-of-the-century Symbolist era in Russia.[23] Even avant-garde designers such as Natan Al'tman and Vladimir Lebedev had been associated with *Mir iskusstva* before 1917, participating in its exhibitions. Conversely, leading *Mir iskusstva* artists such as Lansere, Konstantin Raush-fon-Trauenberg, Valentin Serov, Konstantin Somov, and Serafim Sud'binin had designed important figurines and vases for the Imperial Porcelain Factory, including Somov's gently erotic groups and Sud'binin's renderings of ballet dancers. However unlikely it may seem in retrospect, the World of Art—itself accused of decadence—did much to stimulate the renaissance of porcelain design in the early 1900s; for if, as the critic I. Trotskii wrote in 1924, the late nineteenth century had witnessed a "total lack of principle in artistic activity" at the Imperial Porcelain Factory,[24] then the World of Art raised its level of aesthetic responsibility. Somov was even selected as a candidate for the position of Artistic Director in 1918. Moreover, the World of Art magazine (*Mir iskusstva*, 1898–1904), edited by Sergei Diaghilev, had fostered public interest in porcelain and the applied arts in general, supporting enterprises such as the "Exhibition of Architecture and Industrial Design

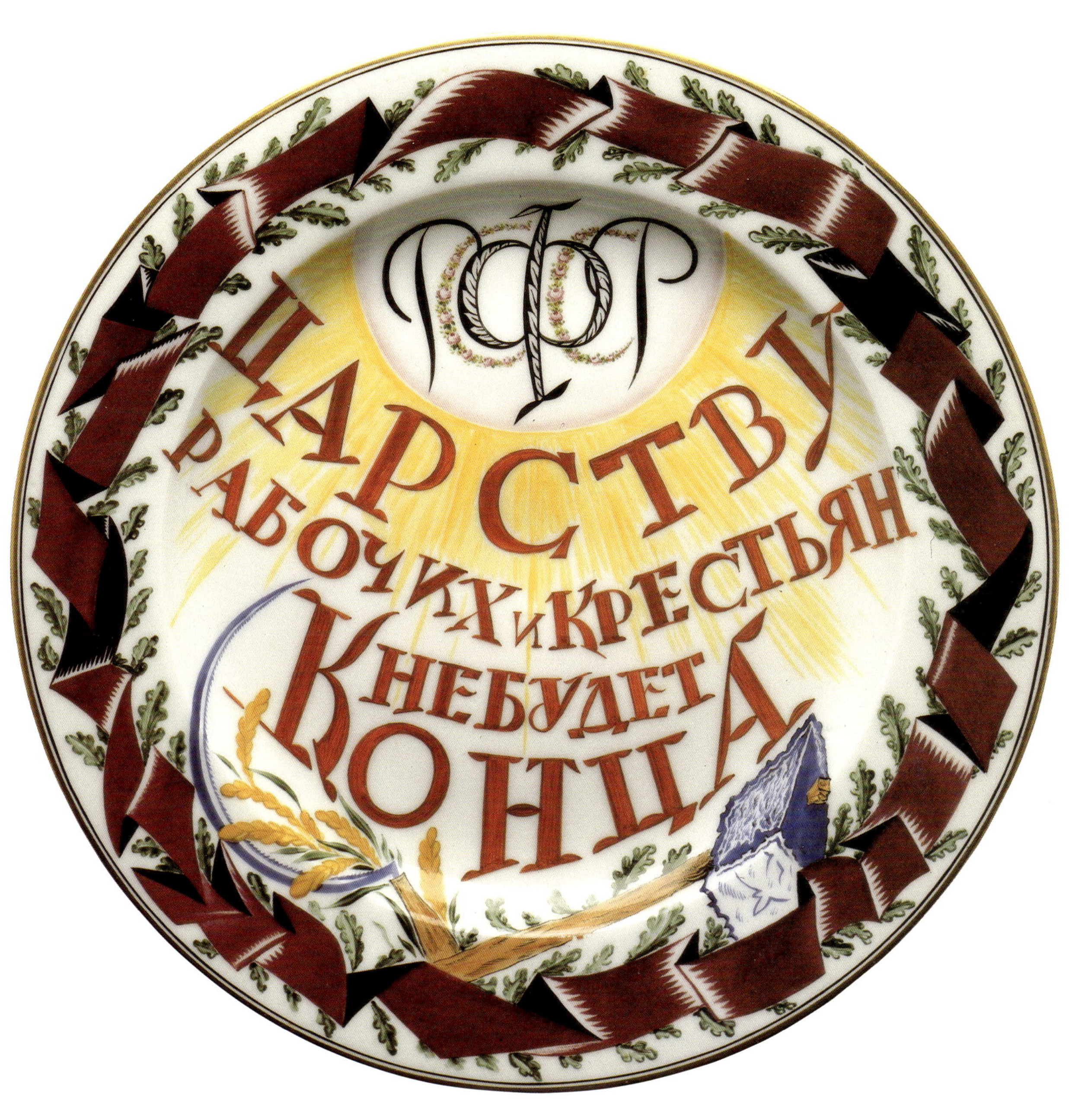

NO. 11

Sergei Chekhonin

Plate, 1922

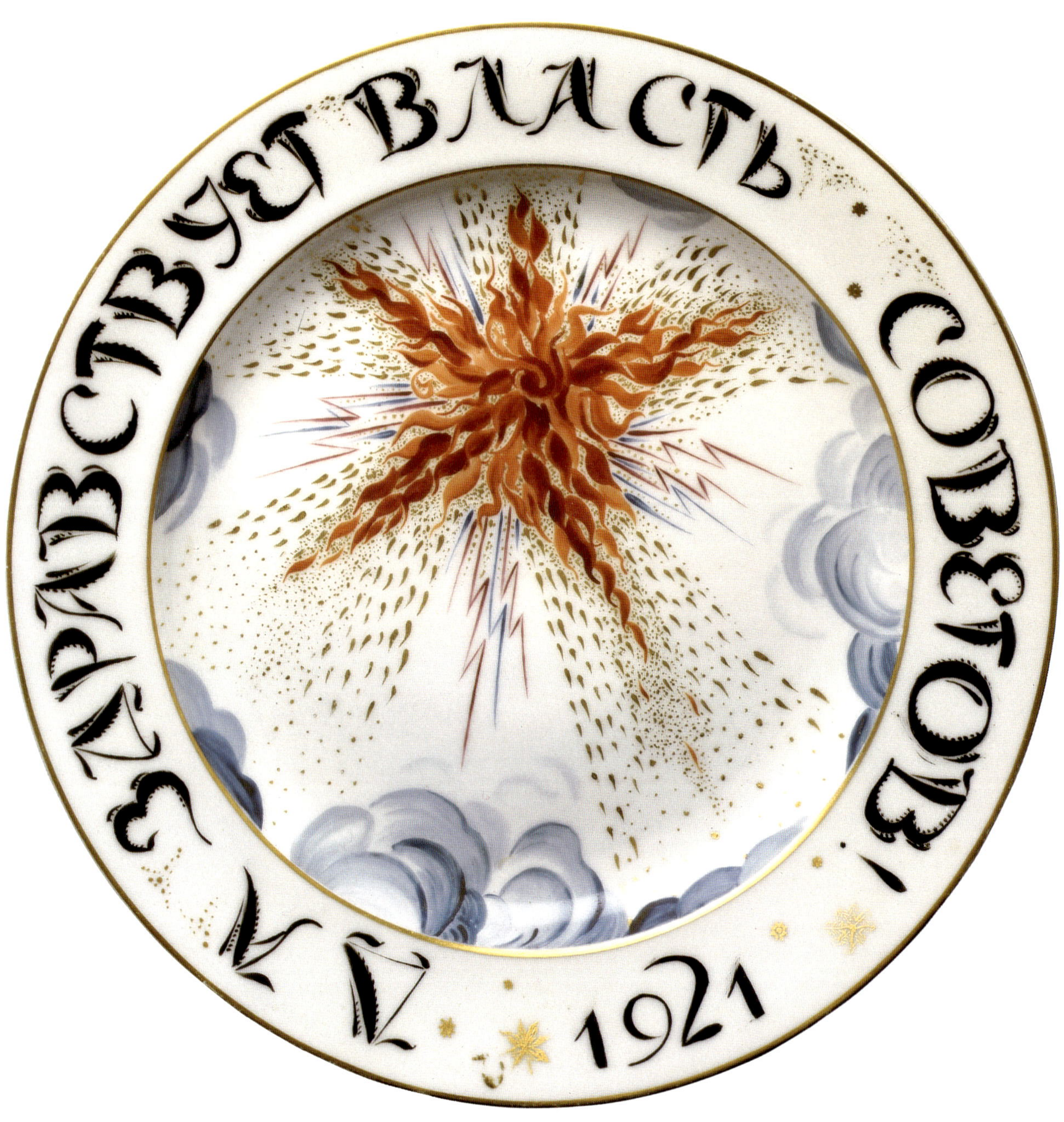

NO. 18

Zinaida Kobyletskaia

Plate, 1921

in the 'New Style'" (Saint Petersburg, 1902–03) and specialist showrooms such as Contemporary Art (Saint Petersburg, 1903), both of which propagated the theory and practice of Art Nouveau. Many Russian national and oriental themes, such as Sadko and the Snow-Maiden, that were interpreted by porcelain artists like Shchekotikhina derive from a *style russe* codified by Lev Bakst, Alexandre Benois (Benua), Ivan Bilibin, and Roerich in the early 1900s. One of the most beautiful plates produced by the State Porcelain Factory in the 1920s carries a rendering of Bakst's costume design for Nijinsky as Iskander in *La Peri* (1911). Roerich was a teacher of Schekotikhina, the designer who most prominently carried Russian themes into the Soviet period. The strong penchant for the "wonderful visions of the East"[25] that were identifiable with the State Porcelain Factory in the 1920s may be explained by its direct connection to the World of Art's cult of Persia, India, Mesopotamia, and Egypt. Exotic pipes by Natal'ia Dan'ko such as *Sun and Moon* (1921) and Dmitrii Ivanov's statuettes of Tamara Karsavina (1920, 1923) might well be interpreted as homages to *Cleopatra*, *Scheherazade*, and other exotic numbers of Diaghilev's Ballets Russes.

The policies of the early State Porcelain Factory, insofar as they are identifiable at present, maintained the aesthetic stance of the World of Art. The factory respected the artisan as much as the artist; encouraged experiment only as a deviation from, and not as a denial of, the classical tradition; and, ultimately, was more interested in "beauty" than in "usefulness." Lunacharskii wrote in 1923:

It is important that food not only be filling, but also tasty. But it is a thousand times more important that a useful object be not only useful and expedient, but also joyful. The dress, the furniture, the porcelain, the home—all must bring joy.[26]

Like their World of Art predecessors, the artists of the factory disputed the conventional division between the "pure" and the "applied" arts, contending that a ceramic piece could be just as "noble" as a studio

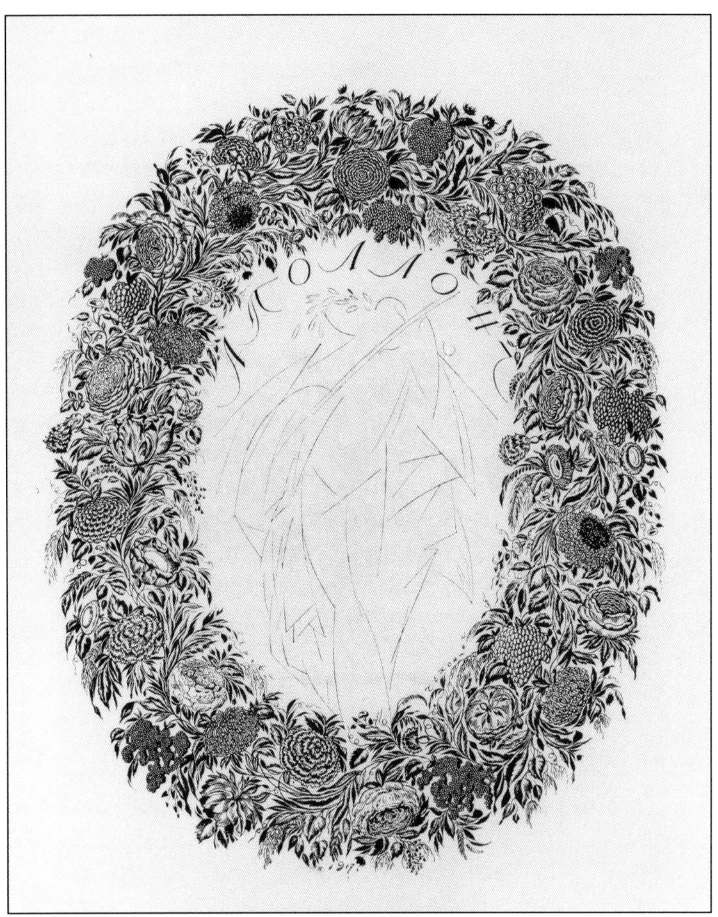

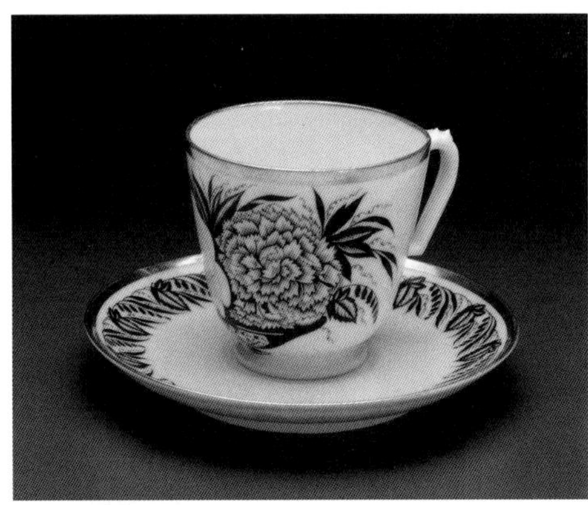

painting.[27] In spite of their ostensibly agitational function, the Soviet cups and plates reveal a much deeper concern with the "independent beauty and perfection of forms."[28] In fact, while most visitors to the exhibition that occasions this catalogue will not be able to read the political slogans, they will be captivated by the aesthetic richness and grace of the wares. Perhaps, in some perverse manner, Gollerbakh was right in arguing that the real agitational message in this kind of porcelain was—or should have been—not in the inscriptions, but simply in the "joyful reception of the beautiful."[29]

Shchekotikhina and her colleagues represented the last wave of the *Mir iskusstva* before its measured elegance was temporarily overshadowed by the geometric abstractions of Suprematism and Constructivism. In 1928, the Constructivist critic Aleksandr Toporkov even observed that "the perfect objects of contemporary applied art, i.e. tables, chairs, lamps, etc., carry no decorations at all."[30] Many avant-garde Soviet artists in various media—Al'tman, Ksen'ia Boguslavskaia, Chashnik, Kandinsky, Ivan Kliun, Vladimir Kozlinskii, Nikolai Lapshin, Anna Leporskaia, Vladimir Lebedev, Malevich, Pavel Mansurov, Liubov' Popova, Jean Pougny (Ivan Puni), Aleksandr Rodchenko, Iosif Shkol'nik, Suetin, and Vladimir Tatlin—experimented with either industrial or domestic porcelain, even if only a few of their prototypes were manufactured. Except for the "unwholesome [and] obscure" Kandinsky,[31] most of these artists applied severe geometric motifs to the ceramic surface, an orientation that has led some historians to speak of a second, or avant-garde, phase in the history of the State Porcelain Factory in the early 1920s. Elena Dan'ko welcomed this development, seeing it as a refreshing

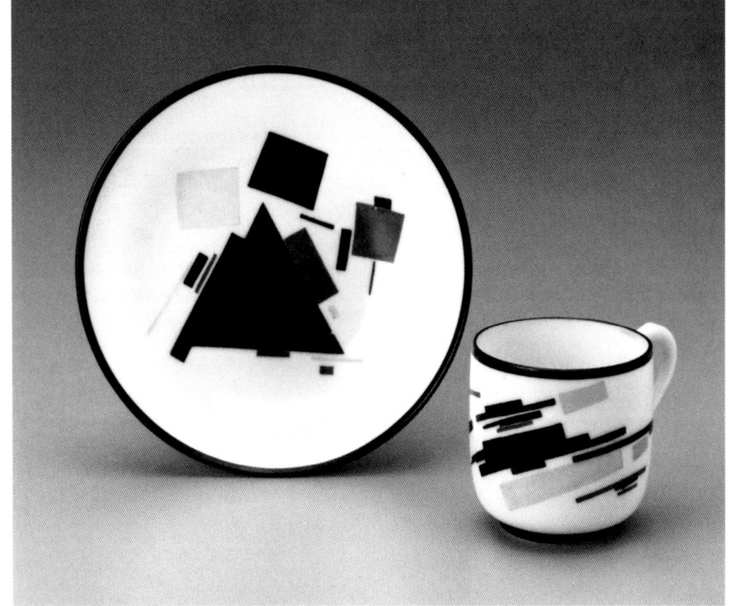

opposition to the ornamental principles of most of the agit-porcelain:

The Suprematists, in the persons of N. Suetin and I. Chashnik, have provided us with a substantial number of examples of Suprematist painting on porcelain. In painting, Suprematism consolidates the individual points of a specific system of consciousness, the ultimate aim of which is to fathom non-objectivity, and as far as porcelain is concerned, this introduces principles that are diametrically opposed to those of the Chekhonin style. A constructive building of colored areas has now replaced the decorative treatment of the surface; the aim of porcelain painting as "decoration" has now been rejected totally.[32]

The reasons for this about-face in the State Porcelain Factory in 1921–22 are many, although, of course, the relevance of Malevich and Suprematism is primary. Obviously, the white of the pure porcelain surface must have appealed to the creator of the *White on White* paintings of 1917–18: "The Suprematist eternal white gives a ray of vision for advancing, encountering no boundary....[It is] pure action [that] has affirmed the sign of the purity of human creative life."[33] Malevich must have regarded porcelain as a propaganda tool that could disseminate the basic Suprematist schemes that he had painted in 1915–16 and then repeated in graphic form in his 1920 booklet *Suprematizm. 34 risunka* (Suprematism: thirty-four drawings). So when he relocated to Petrograd from Vitebsk in 1922, followed by his students, including Chashnik and Suetin (who became head of the Artistic Section in 1932), he turned to the State Porcelain Factory with enthusiasm and curiosity, producing some of the most experimental ceramics of modern times. Many identified the "speechless" code of Suprematism, with its organization of geometric forms in cool, technological progressions and its ostensible call to order, as a strong artistic statement that expressed the universal values of science, industry, and democracy espoused by the October Revolution (see cat. no. 29). "Production art can be only a proletarian art," declared Arvatov in 1926.[34] The Suprematists, there-

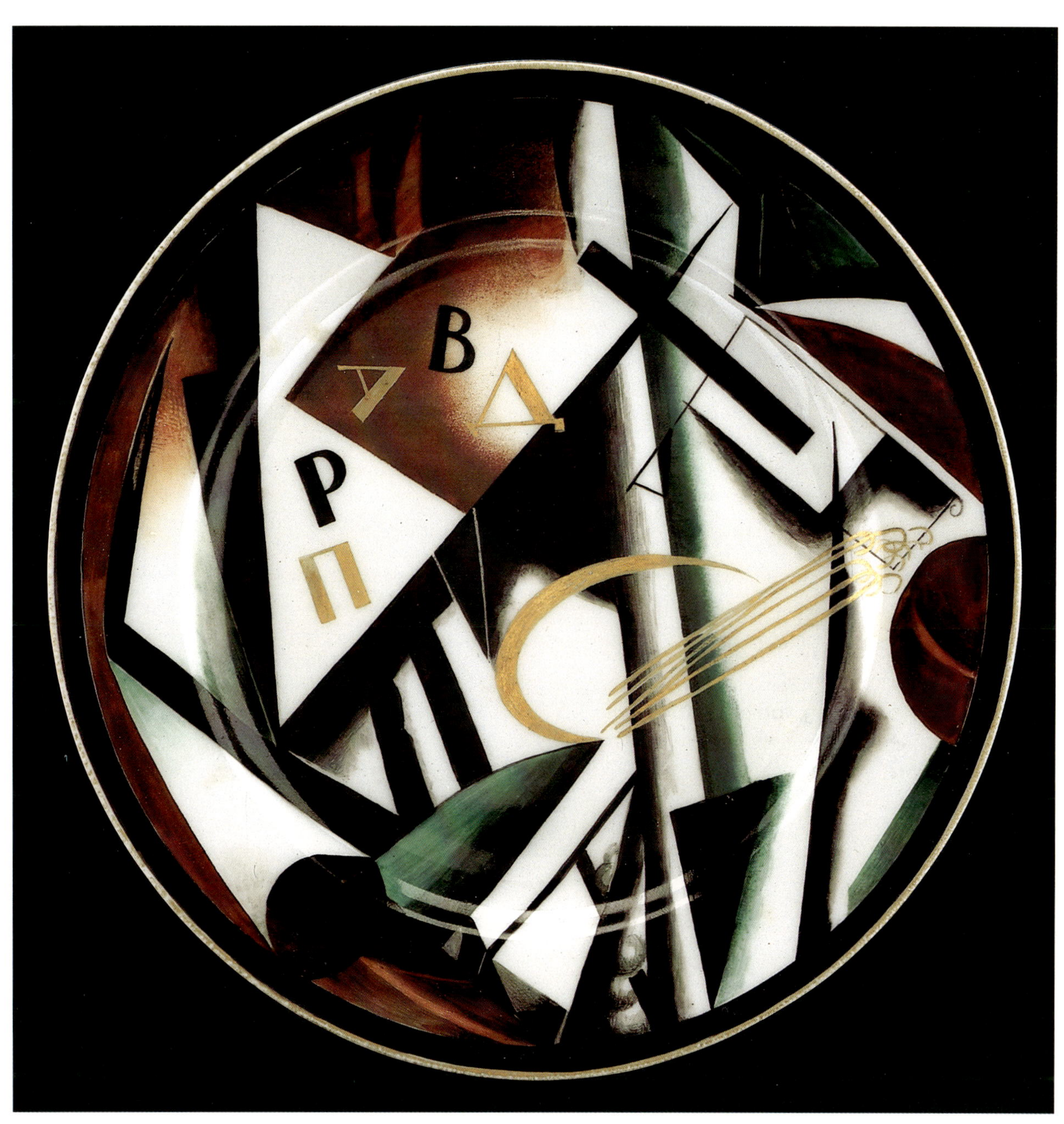

NO. 20
Vladimir Lebedev
Plate called "Pravda,"
n.d.

fore, were not reinterpreting traditional motifs, as Chekhonin or Shchekotikhina were doing, but were offering to the applied arts a new vocabulary of surface configurations and even new material shapes, like a teapot by Malevich (see fig. 5) and an inkwell by Chashnik. Moreover, abstract art was considered by some to be less ambiguous than ornament, appealing to an international and "transcendental" consciousness rather than to a narrowly ethnic and national one. Geometric abstraction, like Constructivism, then, was ideologically more secure (at least for the moment), since it avoided the "metaphysical essence of idealist aesthetics while blazing the trail of consistent artistic materialism."[35]

The Suprematists and the Constructivists (at this juncture, the differences were blurred) also believed in *standartizatsiia*—the creation of prototypes that could be mass-produced by conveyor belt and transfer printing, efficiently and economically—

in direct opposition to the principle of the handmade, hand-painted, small edition supported by the Imperial Porcelain Factory. Similarly, as Liubov' Popova and Varvara Stepanova were affirming in their concurrent dress designs for the new Soviet woman, the abstract, geometric pattern no longer fulfilled an illustrative or narrative purpose and so was not "ruined" by seams, cuts, and tucks—or, in the case of porcelain, by the junctions between center and rim, front and side. Indeed, a major ideological problem with much Soviet porcelain is that the messages, as in Adamovich's "Lenin with Red Star" cup and saucer (cat. no. 2), can be appreciated only if the piece is rotated and observed from all sides, which made the wares unsuitable, even theoretically, for use by the masses in eating and drinking. In some instances, the inscriptions on the porcelain are so deeply incorporated into the design that they are virtually unreadable, as with Chekhonin's plates or even Vil'de's mechanical motifs (see cat. no. 33). In addition, some of the themes of Soviet porcelain decoration were ambiguous or even subversive, such as Adamovich's scene of a city in ruins called "Contemporary Petrograd" (1922), Chekhonin's "Sadness" (1921), Mariia Lebedeva's "Orpheus" (1921), and Shchekotikhina's "Angel and Baby" (cat. no. 24) and "Suffering of Russia" (1921). To the enthusiasts of the new way of life, therefore, Suprematist pottery demonstrated a move from the *rarité* to the multiple edition, from a Russia of quaint bell ringers and Virgin Marys to an international community founded on industrial advancement. As the artist and critic Nikolai Tarabukin declared in 1923:

We're not talking about the rebirth of the forms of studio art as some kind of "industrial" ones, but about the total degeneration of studio art and the birth of a new form of industrial mastery.[36]

The focus of this catalogue is porcelain produced during the first years of the Soviet regime. The cups and saucers, mugs and plates constitute a document of great social importance, narrating a story of tensions

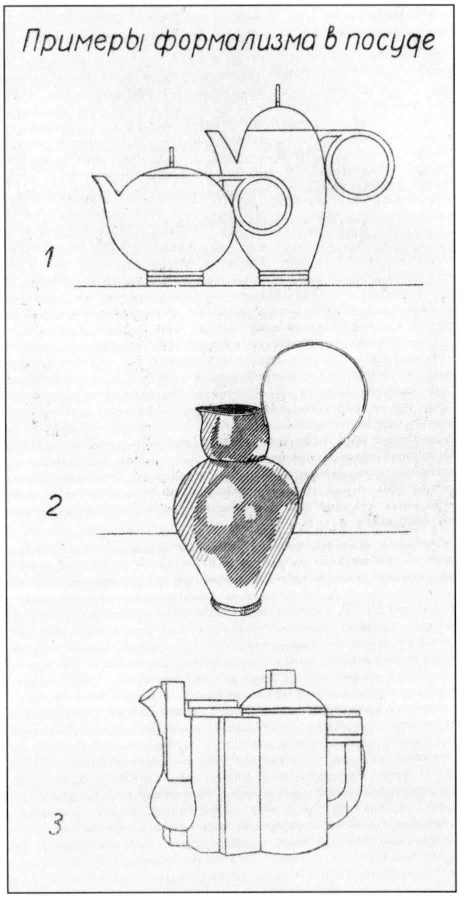

FIGURE 5

"Examples of formalism in ceramics." Photo: A. Filippov, *Khudozhestvennoe oformlenie massovoi posudy* (Moscow, 1932), p. 89, ill. 60. This illustration served to criticize modernism in the decorative arts: Parisian Art Deco, Bauhaus, and Suprematism (exemplified by a teapot by Kazimir Malevich of 1918).

between private and public taste, handicraft and multiple manufacture, and, above all, aesthetic experiment and political dictate. Until the mid-1920s, the flexible, if uneasy, division between individual preference and governmental requirement still pertained; as late as 1934, the year Socialist Realism was ratified as the only legitimate style for Soviet culture, Suetin managed to produce a vase carrying Suprematist elements. Even though Adamovich, Kobyletskaia, Lebedev, and Vil'de ceased to design agit-porcelain, even though Shchekotikhina emigrated in 1923 and Chekhonin in 1928, the State Porcelain Factory still expressed individual and personal aspirations in a surprising array of fanciful motifs, whether Russian fairy tales or celebrations of the Soviet Union's first Five-Year Plan. With the administrative reorganization of the Soviet porcelain industry in 1927, other centers, such as the Dulevo and Dmitrovo factories, began to expand the consumer market, making cheap and cheerful wares with appealing patterns of flowers, birds, and animals. By the early 1930s, the porcelain industry had become so "bourgeois" again that Marxist critics protested in no uncertain terms against a stylistic plurality seemingly irrelevant to the ideological education of the masses in the spirit of communism. The issue was hotly debated at conferences and exhibitions and in a series of key publications, particularly the 1932 collection of essays edited by Aleksei Filippov entitled *Khudozhestvennoe oformlenie massovoi posudy* (The artistic design of mass ceramics). The complaints were many: for example, that "in the artistic design of mass porcelain the pre-Revolutionary legacy has hitherto preserved the absolute domination...of the bourgeois aesthetic of the last third of the nineteenth century";[37] that the continued emphasis on motifs from "Watteau, Boucher, and Fragonard" was alien to the proletarian world view;[38] that Chekhonin, Kandinsky, and Malevich were all the products of a bourgeois society;[39] that the brigades of young designers, "still producing teacups," were removed from the real issues of public life;[40] and even that Malevich's Suprematist teapot was "clumsy, inconvenient, unhygienic, and

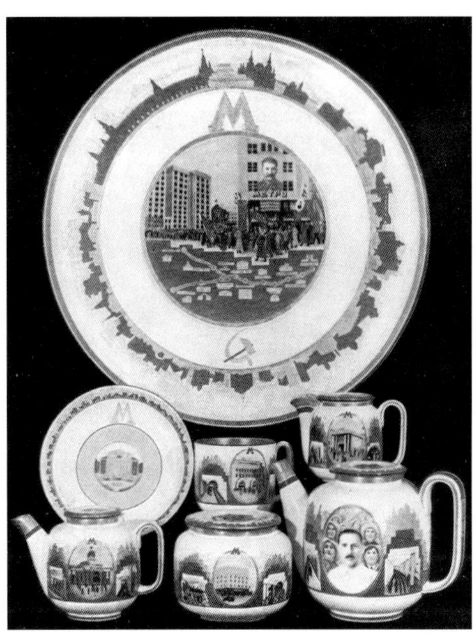

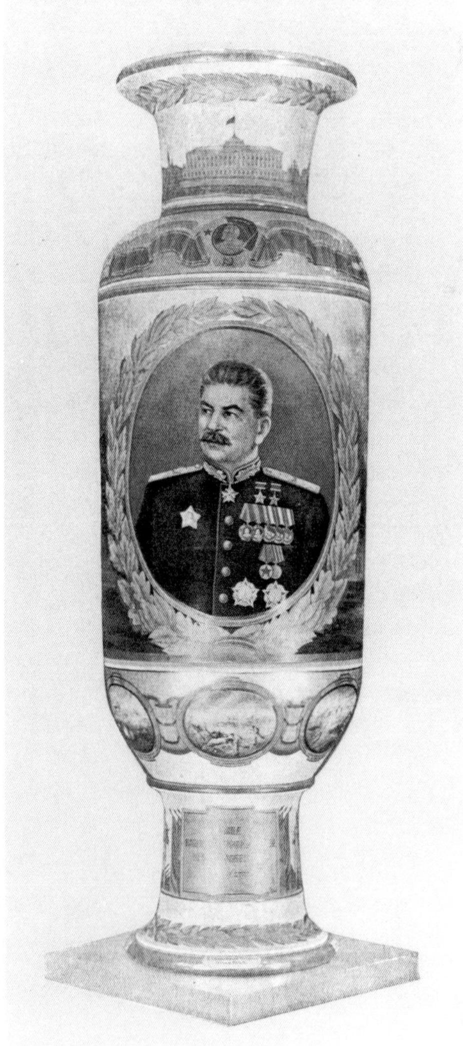

FIGURE 6

State Porcelain Factory, designed by Liudmila Protopopova, *items from a tea service commemorating the first metro in the U.S.S.R.,* porcelain, 1935. Photo: I. Rodin, *La Porcelaine d'arts. Le Catalogue* (Leningrad, 1938), p. 11.

FIGURE 7

State Porcelain Factory, designed by Nikolai Suetin et al., *"victory vase" with portrait of Stalin,* porcelain, 1946. Photo: B. Emme, *Russkii khudozhestvennnyi farfor* (Moscow-Leningrad, 1950), frontispiece.

47

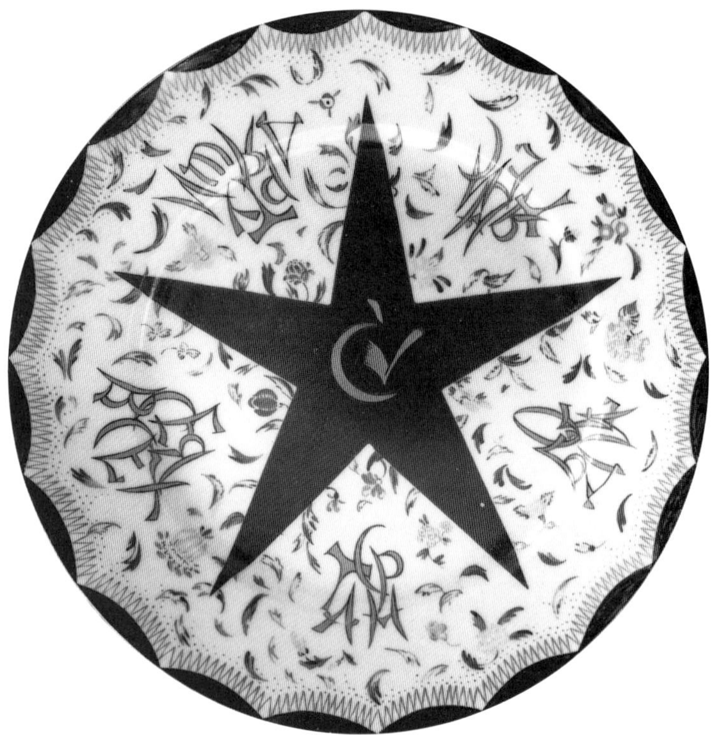

NO. 40
Plate, 1921

inefficient."[41] In calling for a radical reform of the porcelain industry and an end to individual caprice, such criticism signaled the beginning of a new era in Soviet manufacture—of tighter Party control, clearer ideological directive, and immediate subservience to political censorship (see fig. 6).

These bureaucratic measures, however, did not really serve as an antidote to the poisonous charm of the bourgeoisie, and the forthright system of standardized, mass-produced ceramics proposed by Filippov, Natali'a Sokolova, and their colleagues was hardly adopted. On the contrary, they, too, became targets of abuse, criticized for advocating a clinical and "inhuman" style alien to the masses, and the new ideal, the *ampir vo vremia chumy*[42] epitomized in the pompous vases of High Stalinism (often designed by Suetin; see fig. 7), was surely no more efficient or edifying than Chekhonin's platters or Malevich's teapot.

NOTES

1. For information on early Soviet porcelain, including agit-porcelain, see: L. Andreeva, *Sovetskii farfor 1920–1930 gody* (Moscow, 1975); *Art into Production: Soviet Textiles, Fashion and Ceramics, 1917–1935,* exh. cat. Oxford Museum of Modern Art (1984); B. N. Emme, *Sovetskii khudozhestvennyi farfor* (Moscow-Leningrad, 1950); A. V. Filippov, ed., *Khudozhestvennoe oformlenie massovoi posudy* (Moscow-Leningrad, 1932); Eric Gollerbach, *La Porcelaine de la manufacture d'état* (Moscow, 1922); E. F. Gollerbakh and M. V. Farmakovskii, eds., *Russkii khudozhestvennyi farfor: Sbornik statei o gosudarstvennom farforovom zavode* (Leningrad, 1924); *Katalog vystavki izdelii Gosudarstvennogo farforovogo zavoda,* exh. cat. Museum of the State Porcelain Factory, Petrograd (1919); A. K. Lansere, *Sovetskii farfor. Iskusstvo Leningradskogo gosudarstvennogo farforogo zadova imeni M. V. Lomonosova/Soviet Porcelain: Art of the M. V. Lomonosov State Porcelain Factory, Leningrad* (Leningrad, 1974), short summary of text in English; Nina Lobanov-Rostovsky, *Revolutionary Ceramics: Soviet Porcelain, 1917–1927* (New York, 1990); L. Nikiforova, *Russkii farfor v Ermitazhe/Russian Porcelain in the Hermitage* (Leningrad, 1973); *La Rivoluzione in salotto: Porcellane sovietiche, 1917–1930,* exh. cat. Comune di Venezia (Milan, 1988); I. Rodin, ed., *Gosudarstvennyi farforovyi zavod imeni M. V. Lomonosova* (Leningrad, 1938); V. Tolstoi, ed., *Farfor, faians, steklo. Sovetskoe dekorativnoe iskusstvo. Materialy i dokumenty 1917–1932* (Moscow, 1980).
2. According to unsigned introduction in *Katalog vystavki izdelii* (note 1), pp. 10–11.
3. Gollerbach (note 1), pp. 26–27.
4. E. Dan'ko, "Zavod im. Lomonosova (byvsh. Imperatorskii farforvyi zavod 1744–1917)," in Rodin (note 1), p. 28.
5. Dan'ko, ibid., gives the date 1920, but Nikiforova (note 1), p. 26, gives 1921.
6. P. Kerschenzew, *Das schöpferische Theater* (Hamburg, 1922), p. 150.
7. N. Sokolova, "Puti khudozhestvennogo oformleniia massovoi posudy v rekonstruktivnyi period," in Filippov (note 1), p. 14.
8. B. Arvatov, *Iskusstvo i proizvodstvo* (Moscow, 1926), p. 117.
9. This figure is provided by Andreeva (note 1), p. 80.
10. The outlet was in the former Kornilov porcelain store; see Gollerbach (note 1), p. 19.
11. According to Emme (note 1), p. 53.
12. Report from Vaulin to Lunacharskii, Jan. 1918. Quoted in Andreeva (note 1), p. 60.

13. For some idea of Vaulin's ceramic theories, see P. Vaulin, "O khudozhestvennoi keramike," in *Trudy IV s'ezda russkikh zodchikh* (Saint Petersburg, 1911).

14. For some idea of Filippov's ceramic theories, see A. Filippov, *Izraztsovyi nalichnik v Novom Ierusalime* (Moscow, 1917), and "Ratsionalizatsiia i rekonstruktsiia formy massovoi sovetskoi posudy," in Filippov (note 1), pp. 87–139.

15. S. Chekhonin, "Tekhnika rospisi po farforu" in Gollerbakh and Farmakovskii (note 1), p. 34.

16. E. Gollerbakh, "Siuzhety i kharakter zhivopisi po farforu," in Gollerbakh and Farmakovskii (note 1), p. 64.

17. S. Kerkova, *Risovanie po farforu* (Moscow, 1908), p. 3.

18. Most of the documents are contained in the collection compiled by V. Kuchina, *Iz istorii stroitel'stva sovetskoi kul'tury 1917–1918* (Moscow, 1964). For relevant documents on the porcelain industry, see Tolstoi (note 1).

19. From Lenin's decree on monumental propaganda, first published in the newspaper *Izvestiia VTsIK* on Apr. 14, 1918. Reprinted in I. Grabar' et al., *Istoriia russkogo iskusstva* (Moscow, 1957), vol. 11, p. 25.

20. Andreeva (note 1), pp. 62–63, discusses the derivation of some of these maxims.

21. Emme (note 1), p. 55.

22. According to Andreeva (note 1), p. 75.

23. For information on the World of Art, see Janet Kennedy, *The "Mir iskusstva" Group and Russian Art 1898–1912* (Boston, 1977); John Bowlt, *The Silver Age: Russian Art of the Early Twentieth Century and the "World of Art" Group* (Newtonville, Mass., 1979); and Vsevolod Petrov and Alexander Kamensky, *The World of Art Movement* (Leningrad, 1991).

24. I. Trotskii, *Farfor i faians* (Leningrad, 1924), p. 36.

25. Gollerbakh (note 16), p. 38.

26. A. Lunacharskii, "Promyshlennost' i iskusstvo" in *Khudozhestvennyi trud*, 1923, no. 2, p. 7.

27. N. Root, compiler, *Khudozhestvennaia keramika* (Saint Petersburg, n.d.), p. 3.

28. Gollerbakh (note 16), p. 38.

29. Ibid.

30. A. Toporkov, *Tekhnicheskii byt* (Moscow-Leningrad, 1928), p. 196.

31. El [Lissitzky], "Vystavki v Berline," in *Veshch'/Gegenstand/Objet* (Berlin, 1922), nos. 1–2, p. 14.

32. E. Dan'ko, "Novoe Petrogradskogo farforovogo zavoda," in *Khudozhestvennyi trud*, 1923, no. 4, p. 16.

33. K. Malevich, *Suprematizm. 34 risunka* (Vitebsk, 1920), p. 2.

34. B. Arvatov, "Obshchestvo khudozhestvennoi promyshlennosti" in *Vestnik rabotnikov iskusstv* (Moscow, 1926), nos. 1–2, p. 6.

35. M. Ginzburg, "Itogi i perspektivy" (1927), in K. Afanas'ev et al., eds., *Iz istorii sovetskoi arkhitektury 1926–1932 gg.* (Moscow, 1970), p. 82.

36. N. Tarabukin, *Ot mol'berta k mashine* (Moscow, 1923), p. 35.

37. Sokolova (note 7), p. 8.

38. I. Khvoinik, "Meshchanskie tendentsii v oformlenii sovetskoi massovoi posudy" in Filippov (note 1), p. 61.

39. Sokolova (note 7), p. 14.

40. Ibid., pp. 23–24.

41. Filippov (note 1), p. 89.

42. A play on words. Those Soviet citiziens who remember the Stalin era sometimes refer to it by this phrase, the literal meaning of which is the "Empire style during the plague." This is a paraphrase of the title of one of Aleksandr Pushkin's "Little Tragedies," *Pir vo vremia chumy* (*The Feast in the Time of the Plague*, 1832). The neoclassical style formulated under Napoleon was favored during the Stalin era.

Soviet Propaganda Porcelain and the Russian Folk Heritage

ALISON HILTON, *Associate Professor of Art History, Georgetown University*

Fine porcelain plates adorned with workers and soldiers, crossed hammer and sickle, and Revolutionary slogans were surprising, yet strikingly successful, vehicles for expressing the goals of Bolshevism. In the atmosphere of iconoclasm after the October Revolution, tsarist monuments were pulled down, mansions and estates of the gentry were ravaged, and religious and court ceremonies were replaced by mass pageants and parades. Artists collaborated with political leaders in the search for new forms and symbols to create a recognizable, standardized iconography to assert the success and legitimacy of the new regime.[1] Banners, posters, monumental sculptures, speakers' platforms, book kiosks, agitprop trains and boats, dramatic productions, and films were all employed in the urgent effort to spread word of the Revolution throughout the country.

Unlike most other forms of Soviet propaganda art, porcelains were not designed primarily to appeal to the masses; rather, they served to communicate Revolutionary ideals and convey a positive image of the Soviet state to a sophisticated and elite audience. Where the new mass art forms were employed to bring the Revolution to the greatest number of new Soviet citizens, hand-crafted porcelain objects were exhibited abroad, sold for needed hard currency, and displayed in Soviet embassies.

The designs created in the five-year period between 1918 and 1923 fall into three broad groups. One group, including those pieces that adapt styles and images of imperial porcelain, has been described in this volume by Ian Wardropper. In contrast, a second group departs radically from traditional styles to feature designs similar to those of avant-garde posters and street decorations: for example, the nearly abstract "Pravda" plate by Vladimir Lebedev (cat. no. 20), the "Red Army" plate by Mikhail Adamovich (cat. no. 6),

and the striking red and green plate by Natan Al'tman inscribed "Land to the workers" (cat. no. 7). Between these poles, a third group presents a variety of styles evoking traditions other than those of luxury court arts: images inspired by Russian legend and village life (see cat. nos. 17, 23, 30; 8, 27) and forms drawn from icon painting and folk arts (see cat. nos. 16, 24, 39). Most apparent in these works are the artists' efforts to relate Bolshevik themes to the experience of the Russian people.

Posters and other forms of propaganda display a similar range of approaches to the task of persuasion. Propaganda aimed at rural populations, such as a ROSTA (Russian State Telegraph Agency) poster by Lebedev urging peasants to supply food to the Red Army, and posters by Aleksei Radakov, Elizaveta Kruglikova, and Aleksandr Apsit supporting the campaign for literacy and the establishment of village reading rooms, employ familiar settings and motifs from folk costumes, woodcarving, and popular prints to make their messages acceptable.[2] Even agitprop trains, impressive for their speed and dynamic modernity, sometimes displayed frankly folksy decoration, as Vasilii Ermilov's 1921 design of stylized sunflowers and wheat sheaves for "The Red Ukraine" and photographs of the train "The Red Cossack" (fig. 1) show. The latter train and the embroidered banner made for it featured floral motifs from folk embroidery juxtaposed with written slogans and the hammer and sickle.[3]

To understand the role of propaganda porcelains and other arts in the early Soviet period, it is essential to realize that the artists and planners, unlike members of earlier radical art movements such as Futurism, did not advocate the destruction of past art. On the contrary, the establishment of a Commission for Preservation of Monuments and Antiquities was one of the first acts of the Military-Revolutionary Committee in October 1917. The Fine Art

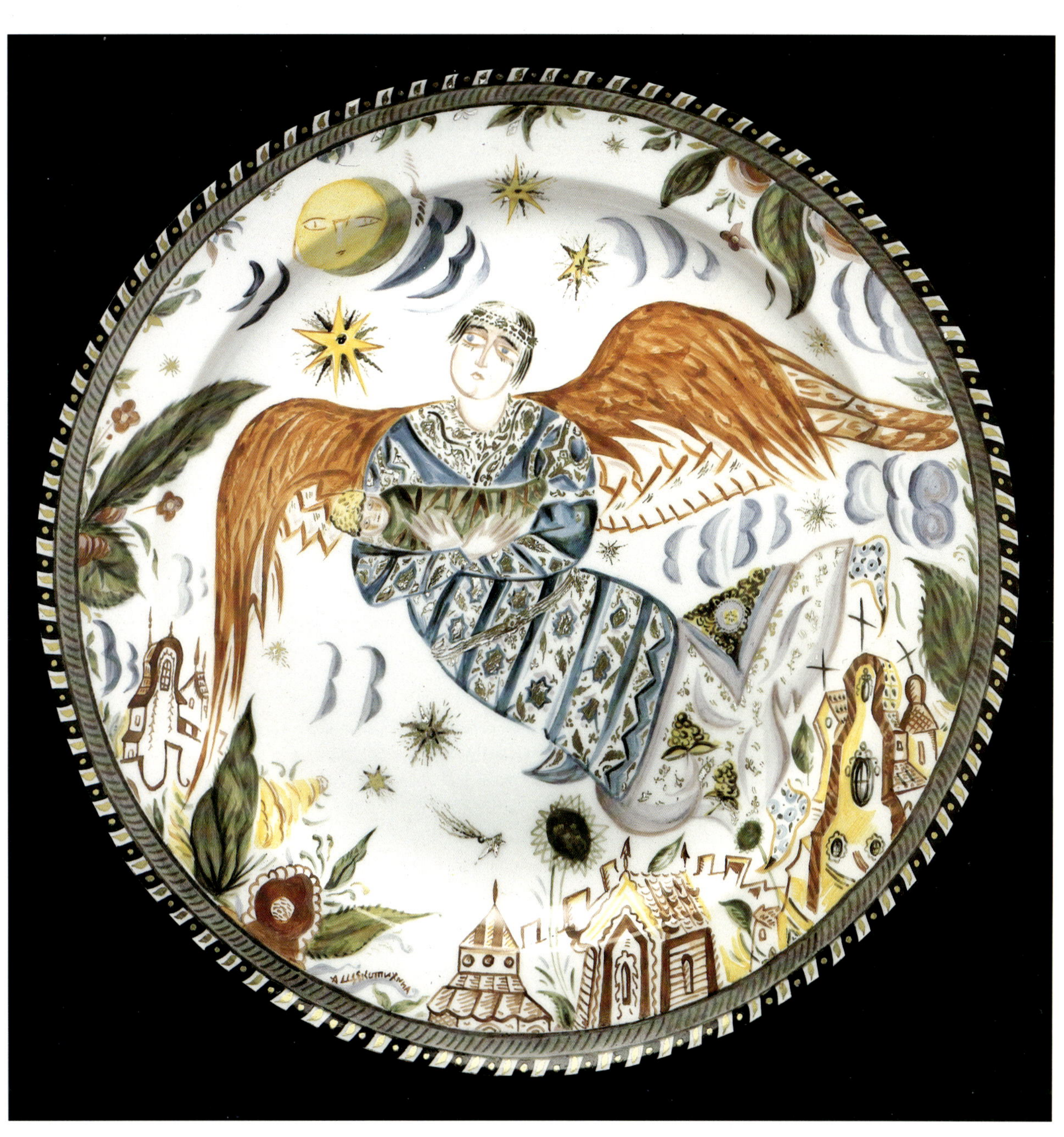

NO. 24
Aleksandra
Shchekotikhina-
Pototskaia
*Plate called "Angel
and Baby,"* 1920

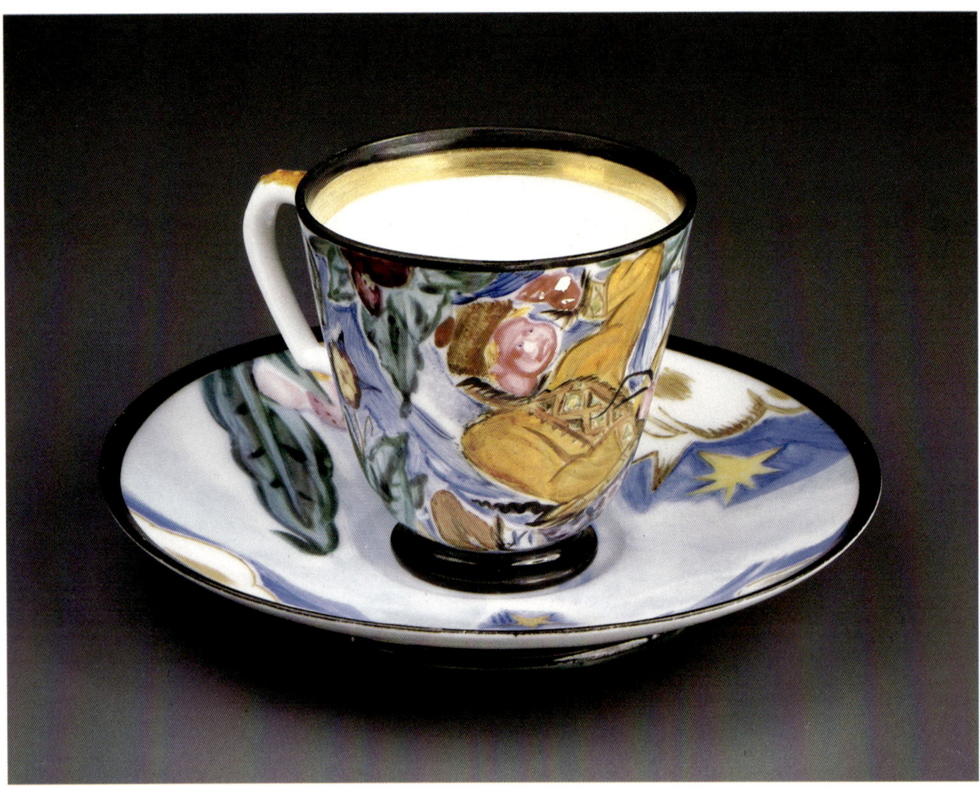

Department of Narkompros, the People's Commissariat for Enlightenment, included artists and art scholars of all stylistic and theoretical interests.

The group of propaganda plates representing Russian decorative traditions other than those of the Imperial Porcelain Factory is significant because it calls into question the conventional separation of "elite" and "popular" art. Although porcelain was too expensive to be purchased by most people, those who saw these works could appreciate the artists' interest in folk and popular culture. Adapting folk-art motifs and decoration to dishes required changes to porcelain decorative conventions. In some pieces, the usual treatment of center and rim of the plate as separate entities was altered to preserve the integrity of a human figure or a familiar scene; inscriptions are simple and blocklike rather than calligraphic, or are lacking altogether. The imagery in these pieces makes a statement about the relationship of the state to the people quite different from the one implied by the more "imperial" or abstract forms.

The use of Russian "folk" elements in Soviet porcelain, however, was neither particularly revolutionary nor unprecedented.

A fashion for the *style russe* had affected architecture and the decorative arts for some four decades before the October Revolution. The influential workshops at Abramtsevo and Talashkino produced, exhibited, and sold furniture, ceramics, and embroidered and printed textiles not only in Moscow but in major European cities. By the turn of the century, several firms specialized in luxury goods of silver, bronze, enamel, and silk brocade, as well as porcelain, based on designs from medieval Muscovy and from a variety of folk arts.[4] The Kuznetsov firm in Moscow, for example, made porcelain plates decorated with "old Russian" and "folk" cross-stitch designs for members of the imperial family (see fig. 2); and the Kornilov Brothers factory in Saint Petersburg made plates, coffee services, figurines of peasants, and even porcelain imitations of sixteenth-century metal *kovshy* (ceremonial dippers), many for export to the United States.[5] The pre-Revolutionary manufacturers often combined styles from several sources on one piece and applied designs traditionally used for specific materials to different media, a practice that distressed many serious students of icons, historical Russian ornament, and folk art, such as the eminent critic Vladimir Stasov and the artist Ivan Bilibin.[6] The English writer and photographer Netta Peacock, however, explained the eclectic style of the "new Russian decorative art" in a more positive way:

So thoroughly have they impregnated themselves with the spirit of legend and fairy-tale as still told by the poet-peasant... that their designs are distinctly national both in feeling and colour. This new movement is...an exaltation of the popular genius.[7]

In the Soviet period, too, artists who became fascinated with icons and folk arts, and who saw their potential for decorating porcelain and communicating political messages, rarely made distinctions among the various sources of styles and images; they were artists rather than scholars. Models were readily available in early twentieth-century Russia. The icons integral to Russian Orthodox worship were ubiquitous (and icons and churches did not disappear with the Revolution); *lubki* (sing. *lubok*), popular prints reproduced by engraving or lithography, were still sold cheaply at street kiosks; and brightly painted tin trays, wooden dishes, toys of all descriptions, and glazed majolica dishes were displayed in shops and open-air markets. In the 1910s, artists like Natal'ia Goncharova, Mikhail Larionov, Kazimir Malevich, Il'ia Mashkov, and Aleksandr Shevchenko had discovered the "simple, unsophisticated beauty of the *lubok*" and saw the "primitive art forms—icons, *lubki*, trays, signboards" as fresh and vigorous sources that could revitalize art.[8] While the Neoprimitivists valued icon and folk-art styles for their expressive possibilities, they also used them to emphasize Russianness and to assert their independence from European academic traditions. As Goncharova declared, "The art of my country is incomparably more profound and important than anything that I know in the West."[9] Malevich linked his discovery of icons and folk arts to his understanding of the "emotional" content of art and, by implication, to the expressive power of form and color independent of representation.[10]

While avant-garde artists were interpreting popular sources freely, officially sponsored exhibitions of icons and folk arts and crafts were introducing authentic Russian arts to the public. Before and after the Revolution, commissions of scholars and artists were charged with preserving folk-art objects and teaching traditional styles and techniques so that local art forms might continue to develop in contemporary "folk-art industries." Under the authority of Narkompros, specialized workshops and factories producing ceramics, textiles, metalwork, wooden articles, and porcelain were reorganized. Professional artistic directors collaborated with workers to

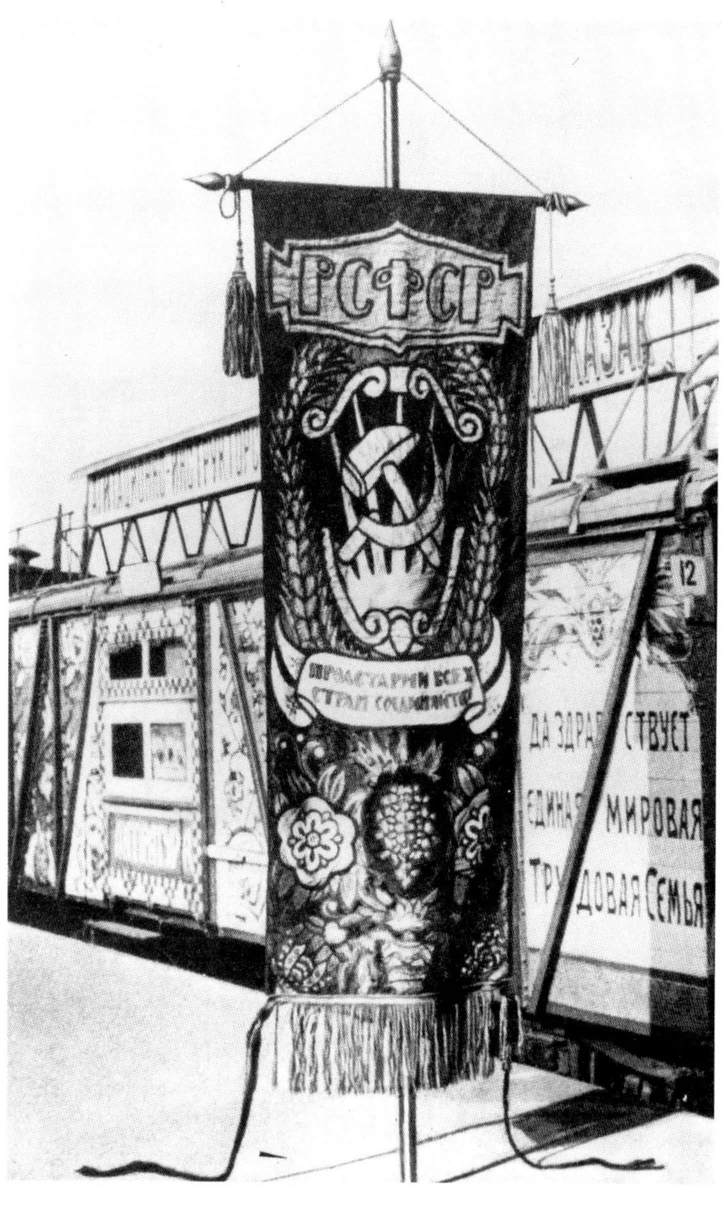

FIGURE 1

"The Red Cossack" agitprop train and banner (detail), 1920. Photo: Michael Guerman, *Art of the October Revolution* (Leningrad and New York, 1979), no. 337.

53

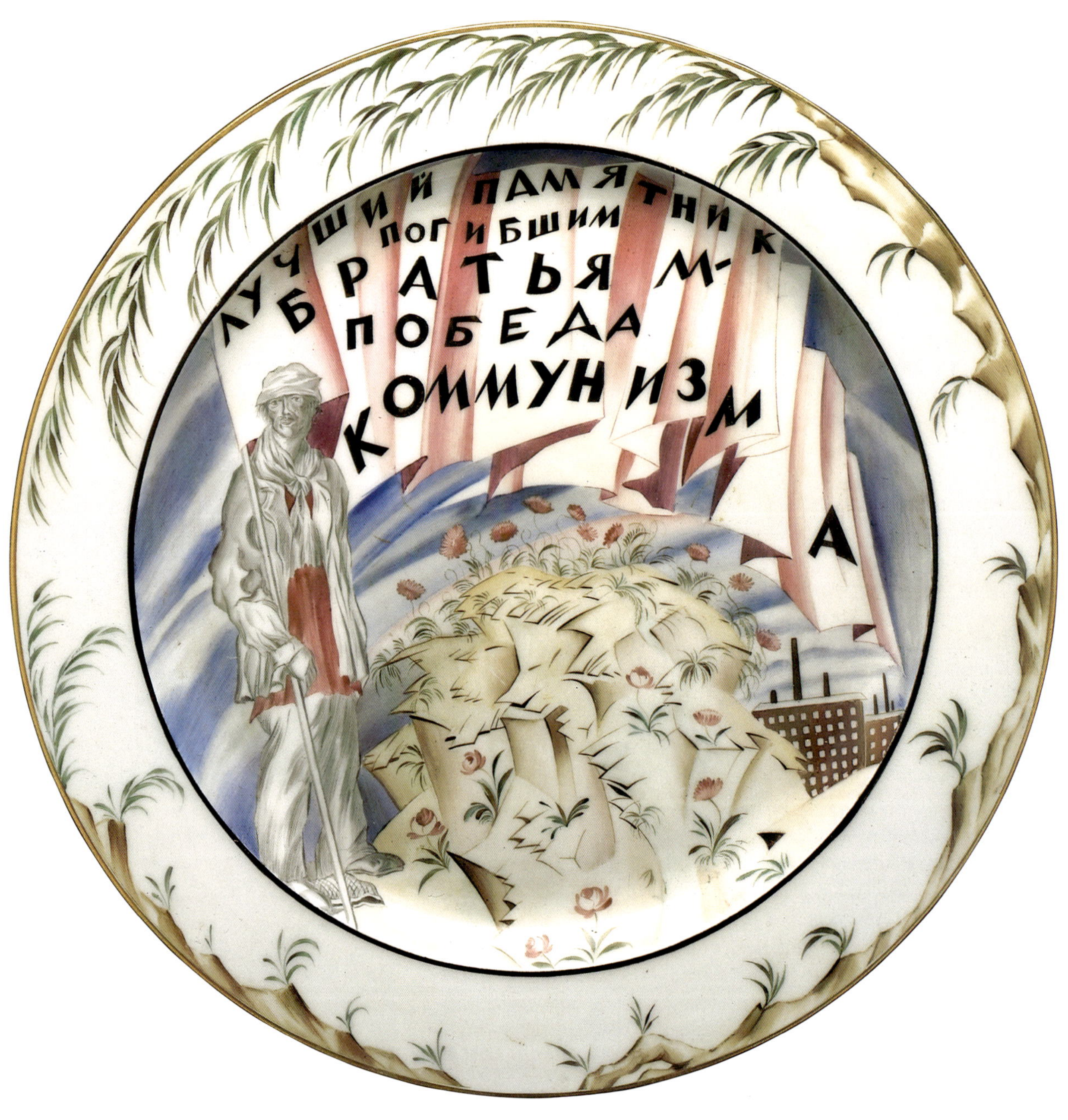

NO. 16

Alisa Golenkina

Plate, 1920

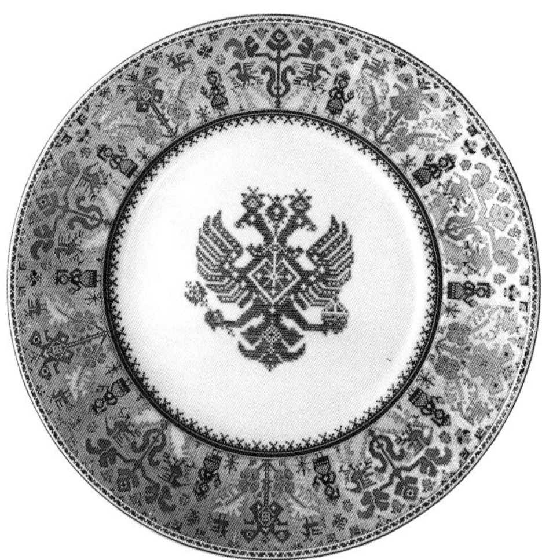

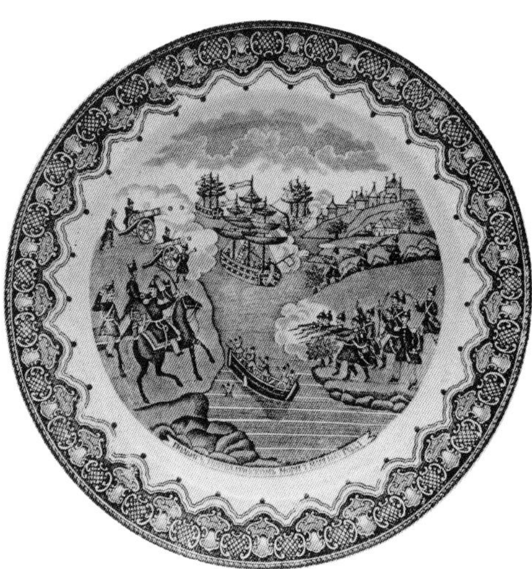

continue production and training and to exhibit and sell their wares abroad, following a 1919 decree outlining measures to promote the applied arts.[11] The importance of old Russian and folk-art references in decorative arts and painting of the pre-Revolutionary period, and the range of attitudes toward these sources, helps to explain the prominence of these forms in early Soviet applied arts. The "folk" styles in porcelain emerged not only out of the propaganda artists' search for forms appealing to popular tastes, but also out of an already established visual vocabulary that could be used for many different purposes.

Among the artists who worked with Sergei Chekhonin at the State Porcelain Factory, a few, such as Rudol'f Vil'de, had prior experience in porcelain painting and continued to rely on traditional techniques. Others, Aleksandra Shchekotikhina-Pototskaia among them, were trained in painting, sculpture, or graphic arts, and they were more inclined to look to a variety of sources, including the folk arts, for models. Some artists, particularly Chekhonin, also experimented with the broad, spontaneous brushstrokes used by painters of cheaper porcelain and majolica dinnerware in a technique known as *agashka* (see cat. no. 9).[12]

Obvious stylistic sources for porcelain were ceramics, including architectural and stove tiles and common utensils of majolica or inexpensive porcelain. Most of these domestic ceramics were made in a group of villages south of Moscow collectively known as Gzhel'. Gzhel' was famed since the eighteenth century for majolica tableware decorated with polychrome enamel colors depicting animals, birds, and scenes from village or military life, and, by the early nineteenth century, for its pitchers and plates of semifaience (a near-white, even, and durable ceramic ware) with garlands, inscriptions, and often small, modeled genre figures, glazed with lustrous cobalt. Later, several factories in the area produced faience and porcelain dishes with complex illustrations of military campaigns (see fig. 3), topographical views, and luxuriant floral ornament imitating the styles of the Imperial Porcelain Factory.[13] However, at the end of the century, ceramics firms employing machine processes drew away much of the market, and the Gzhel' workshops declined. After World War I and the Revolution, the Gzhel' area was desolate, but, in keeping with the 1919 decree on the applied arts, efforts were made to resurrect its potteries. A major conference on ceramics production was held in the summer of 1920; members of cooperative workshops studied the best products of earlier years and worked to develop efficient new techniques.[14] There was never any question of competing with the State Porcelain Factory, but the coexistence of efforts to adapt and improve ceramics in the spheres of both fine and common applied arts was in itself significant.

Other sources for the exuberant floral ornaments (see cat. nos. 9, 34) were tin trays from Zhostovo painted with floral designs on black or red grounds; enam-

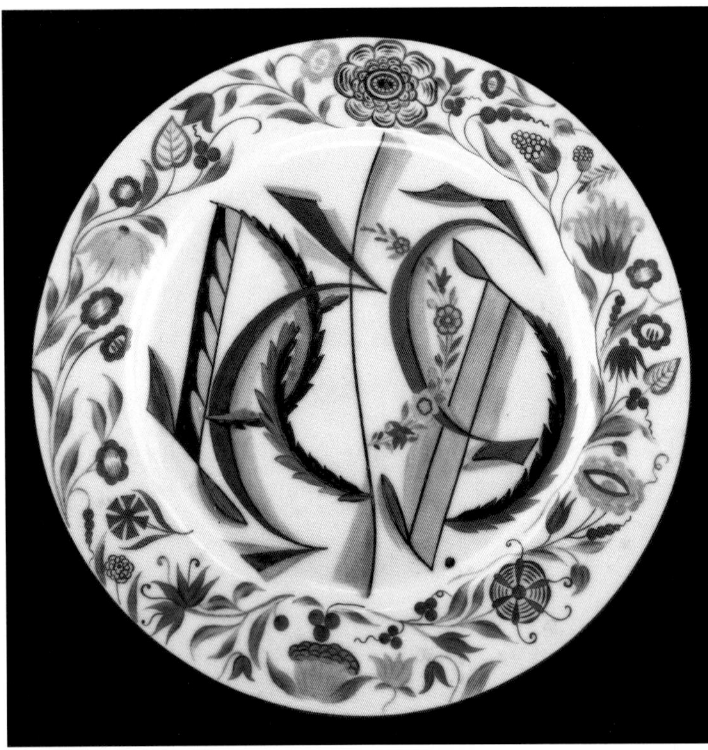

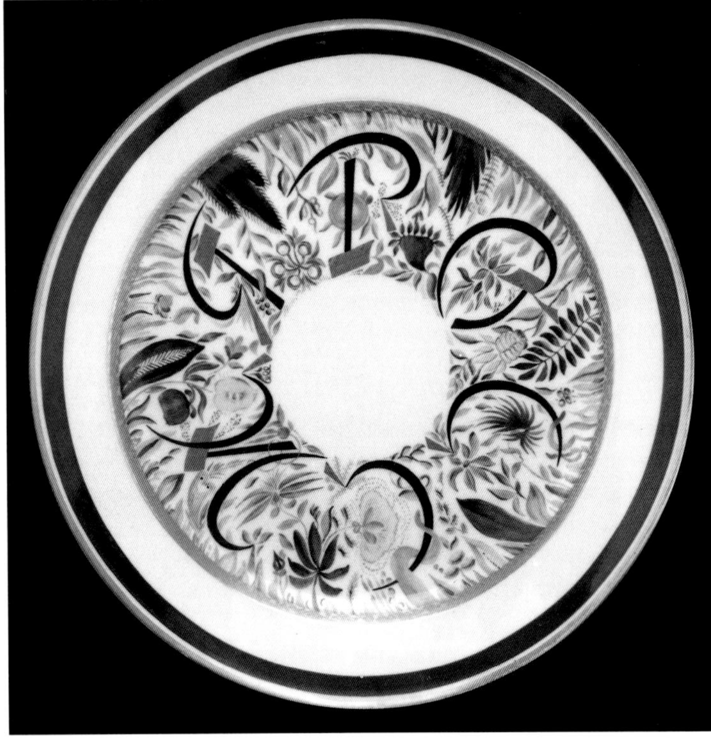

eled copper brooches, pendants, and decorative boxes from Rostov; and folk painting on wooden dishes, distaffs, cradles, cupboards, and even interior walls of peasant houses. The styles of floral borders on some plates (see, for example, cat. nos. 15, 39) are closer to paintings on wood than ceramics; and the ornaments on the hammer and sickle of a plate by Mikhail Adamovich (cat. no. 3) vividly recall stylized rosettes carved and painted on horse yokes and other tools. Geometric motifs based on embroidery and wood-carving figure less prominently here than in *style russe* porcelains of the late nineteenth century, with the striking exception of Shchekotikhina-Pototskaia's "Bell-Ringer" plate (cat. no. 27). This character, a peasant sowing grain on a plate by Veniamin Belkin (see cat. no. 8), and Shchekotikhina-Pototskaia's young "Wool Winders" (see cat. no. 26) suggest the styles of Neoprimitivist paintings, but they may be more directly related to forms such as *lubki* and carved and painted wooden utensils and toys.

Many types of folk art recorded social customs and current events: in the early nineteenth century, soldiers and "cavaliers" in Napoleonic costume frequently appeared on distaffs and as toy figures; and, in mid-century, toys made in the Volga region and the Urals reproduced contemporary fashions of western Russia and Poland, brought to these regions by political exiles. In the Soviet era, professional artists worked with peasant woodcarvers, embroiderers, and other village craftspeople to introduce new themes and personages such as the Red Army soldier into the repertoire of designs (see fig. 4). The inherent flexibility of folk arts, their ability to include new elements in traditional forms, was welcomed and exploited by the planners and administrators of developing folk- and applied-arts industries.[15]

Direct experience of life in the Russian countryside and provincial towns was important for some artists. Shchekotikhina-Pototskaia traveled in northern Russia as an art student, visiting areas settled largely by Old Believers, decandants of families exiled from the Novgorod and Moscow regions in the seventeenth century for their rejection of

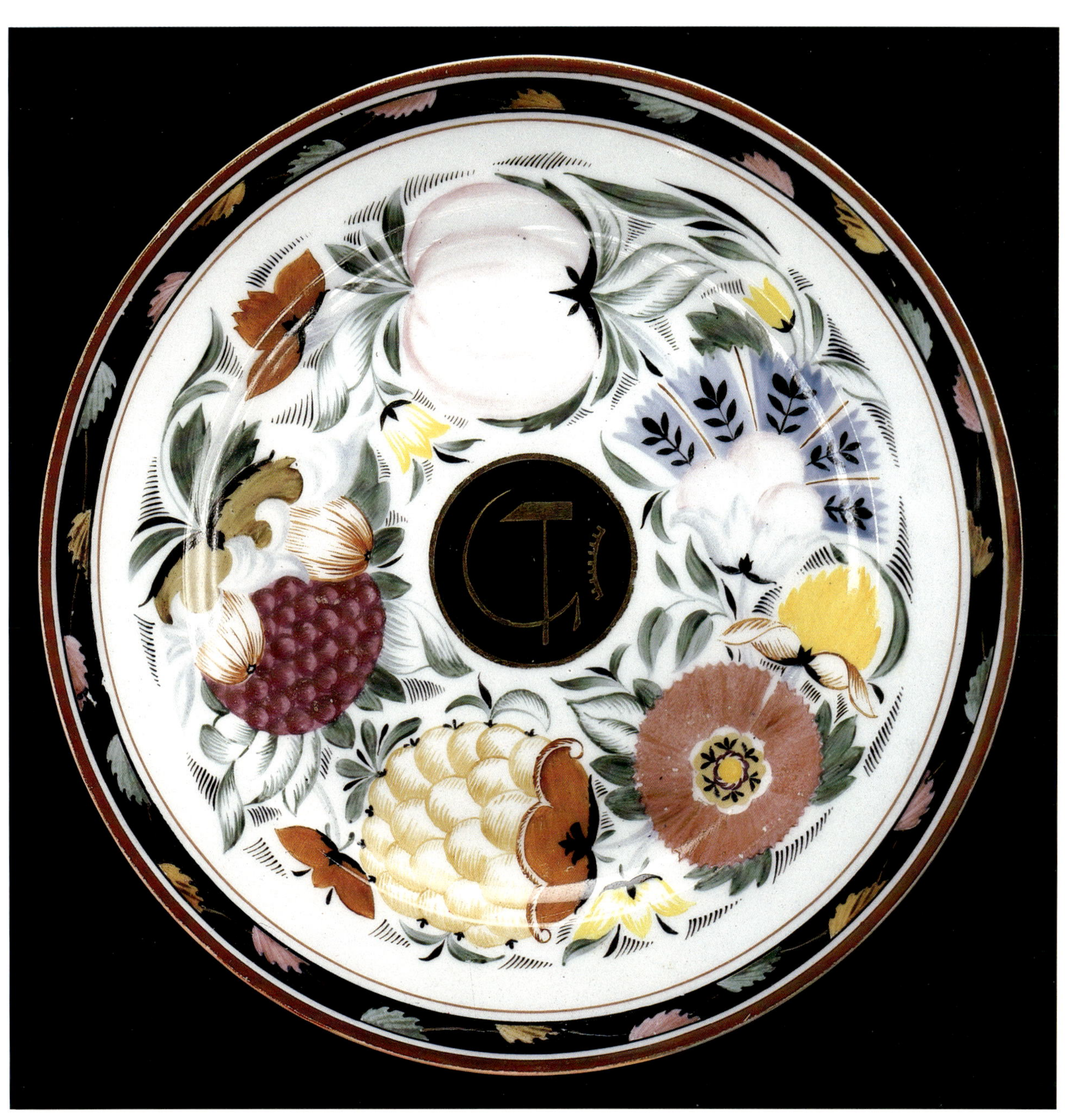

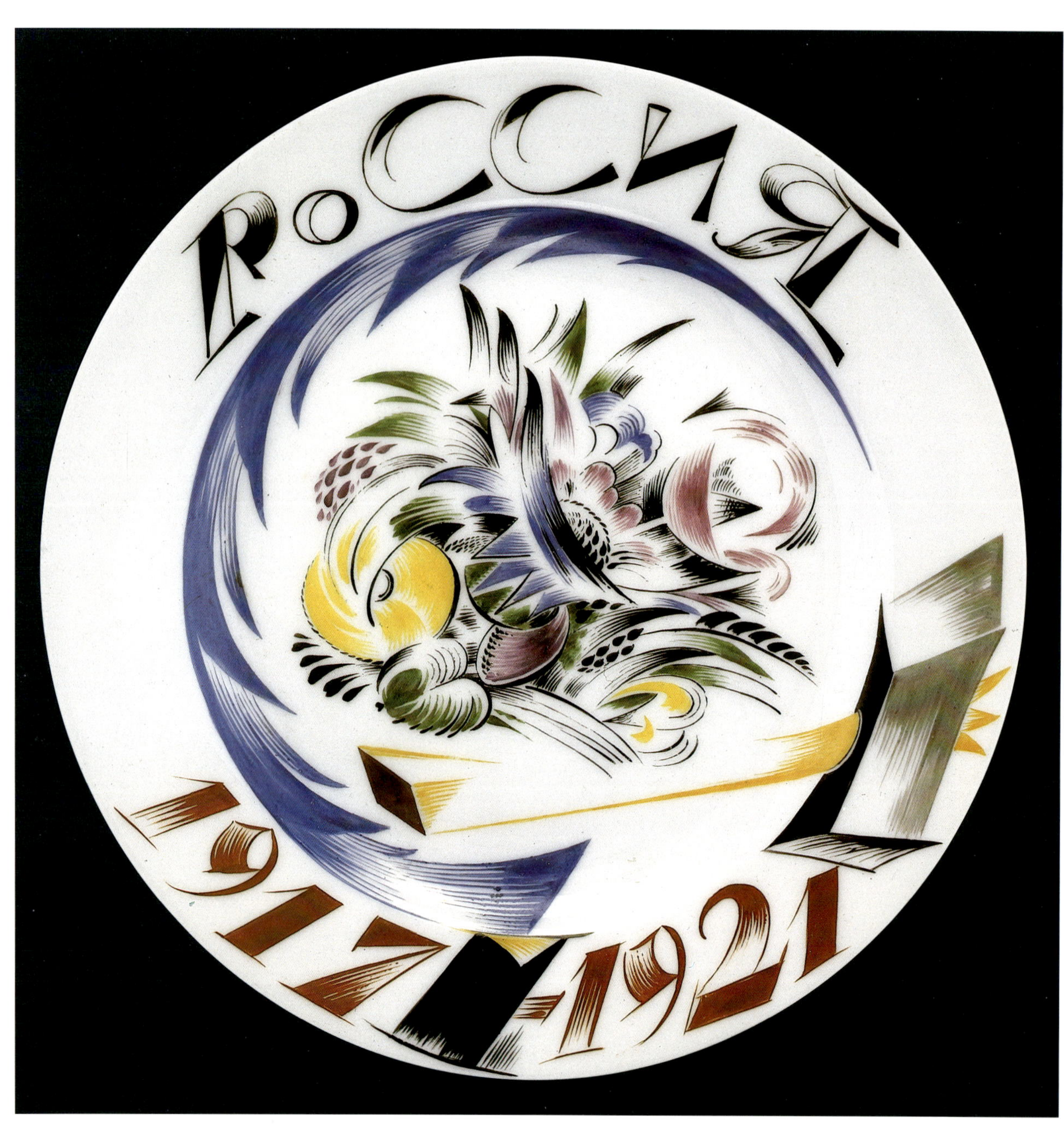

NO. 34
Attributed to
Rudol'f Vil'de
Plate, 1921

58

secular authority. From an Old Believer family herself, Shchekotikhina deeply appreciated the styles of icon and manuscript painting still evident in the painted wooden utensils characteristic of Vologda and Arkhangelsk provinces.[16] In these regions, traditional social roles and village activities were carried into the twentieth century. The festive atmosphere of the "Wool Winders" plate, for instance, indicates a social occasion rather than a commonplace domestic task. Village women gathered in the evenings to spin flax or wind wool and talk or sing, and they were usually joined by men and boys with guitars or accordions (see fig. 5); these informal gatherings, often depicted on distaffs and other domestic tools, were opportunities for young people to meet and court.[17] The figures on this plate wear outfits combining village and town features: the young man wears a peasant's striped shirt with embroidered borders and a dandyish waistcoat; the woman wears the embroidered blouse, headdress, and gold earrings and crucifix of a well-to-do peasant with a dress designed like an updated *sarafan*, a traditional costume, with a nipped-in waist. Their faces show coy smiles and meaningful glances. The nostalgic image, reassuring the viewer that such traditional patterns of life would continue under the new regime, requires no inscription.

Finally, Russian icons and legends gave rise to elements of style and imagery. A plate by Alisa Golenkina, inscribed "The best monument to our fallen brothers is the victory of communism" (cat. no. 16), quotes icon style in its depiction of the rugged hill between the specter of a dead revolutionary and a distant factory. In contrast, Vasilii Timorev's plate inscribed "He who is not with us is against us" (cat. no. 30) depicts Saint George slaying a dragon, one of the most cherished subjects in traditional religious art, in a style with little debt to icons. The knight, in reddish armor, bears a shield with the hammer and sickle as a coat of arms and strides over the flaccid white body of the monster, an unmisable reference to the Reds beating the counterrevolutionary Whites, an interpretation reinforced by the red star rising over the horizon.

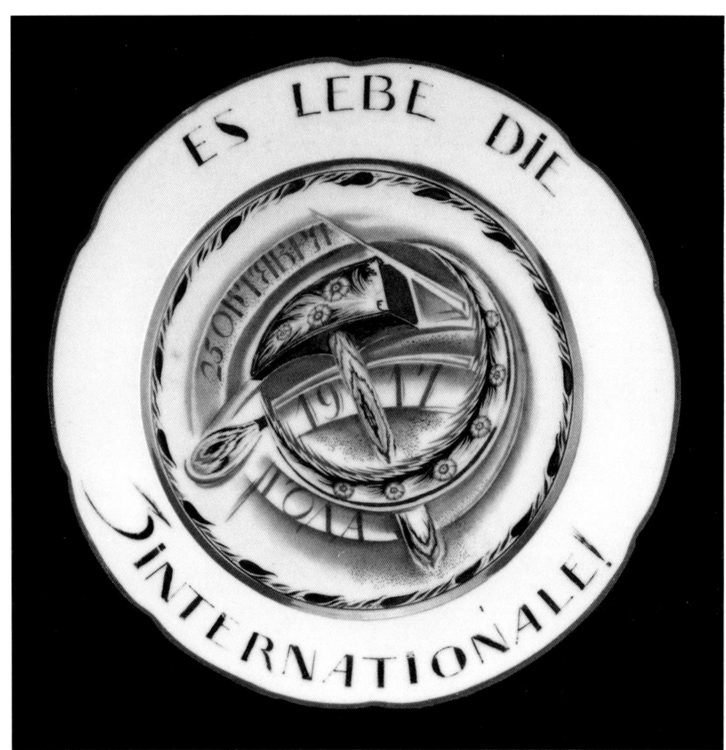

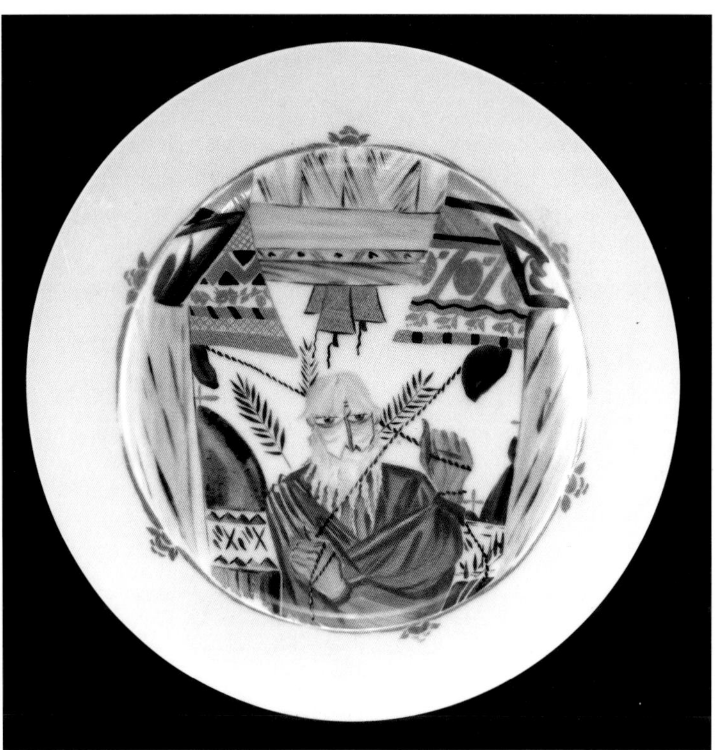

Top
NO. 3
Mikhail Adamovich
Plate, 1921

Bottom
NO. 27
Aleksandra
Shchekotikhina - Pototskaia
Plate, 1921

Legend and fantasy inspired plates in dramatically different styles by Golenkina (cat. no. 17) and Shchekotikhina (cat. no. 24). In Golenkina's plate, an inscription in German, "We inflame the whole world with the fire of the Third International," surrounds a torch-bearing rider on a winged horse flying above classical ruins engulfed in flames and smoke. The central motif appeared three years earlier on the cover of the Soviet calendar for 1919, in which the horse and rider are surrounded by stylized sun rays and framed by linked signs of the zodiac.[18] The image points to a conflation of ancient, heroic sources: the Greek myth of Belerophon and Pegasus, the Russian icon of the Archangel Michael flying on a winged horse over a burning city, and *lubki* portraying the legendary heroes, *bogatyri,* of Kievan Rus'.[19] These all express the themes of superhuman powers and the cleansing force of destruction.

In contrast, Shchekotikhina's plate with an angel holding a swaddled infant, flying above a vista of Russian churches and towers, surrounded by stars, clouds, flowers, and a smiling yellow sun, conveys a feeling of gentle protectiveness. The artist decorated a square platter with the same design,[20] and a cup and saucer with similar motifs: a horse and rider leaping over a river amidst stars, clouds, and a human-faced sun (cat. no. 23). The composition and handling of paint—with the large central figure and smaller forms scattered loosely over a white ground, and the combination of loose brushstrokes in the angel's wings, the complex patterning of the dress, and the calligraphic contours of the architecture, foliage, and facial features—are reminiscent of the styles of northern Russian icons, manuscripts, and folk painting on wood. Shchekotikhina's guardian angel resembles a *sirin,* a bird-like creature with a woman's face that often graced distaffs and other painted objects (see fig. 6).

Shchekotikhina's interest in old Russian themes was stirred by her family background and reinforced by her contact with Nikolai Roerich (Rerikh) and Ivan Bilibin at the School of the Society for Encouragement of the Arts in Saint Petersburg, where she studied between 1908 and 1915. Both men were deeply interested in the arts of the Russian north, aiming to give them new artistic expression through paintings, book illustration, and theatrical design. Even after Shchekotikhina had studied in Paris, exhibited with the cosmopolitan World of Art group, and begun to work with Chekhonin at the State Porcelain Factory, her fascination with folk art and the Russian past continued. A versatile artist, Shchekotikhina also designed plates with modernist forms and Bolshevik themes (like her "Commissar" plate, cat. no. 28), but she clearly attached special importance to images from Russian folk life and legend. She collaborated for many years with Ivan Bilibin, whom she married, doing costume and set designs for productions of Russian operas, both in the Soviet Union and while living abroad, and her porcelains themselves suggest the broad, colorful effects of theater on a small scale. One scholar characterized Shchekotikhina's contribution to porcelain painting as giving it "an expressionistic *lubok* quality,"[21] perhaps a way of conveying her confident, expansive treatment of the medium.

In the diversity of styles of early Soviet porcelain, we can see a shared awareness of the value of traditional forms for the art of the new society. The apparent spontane-

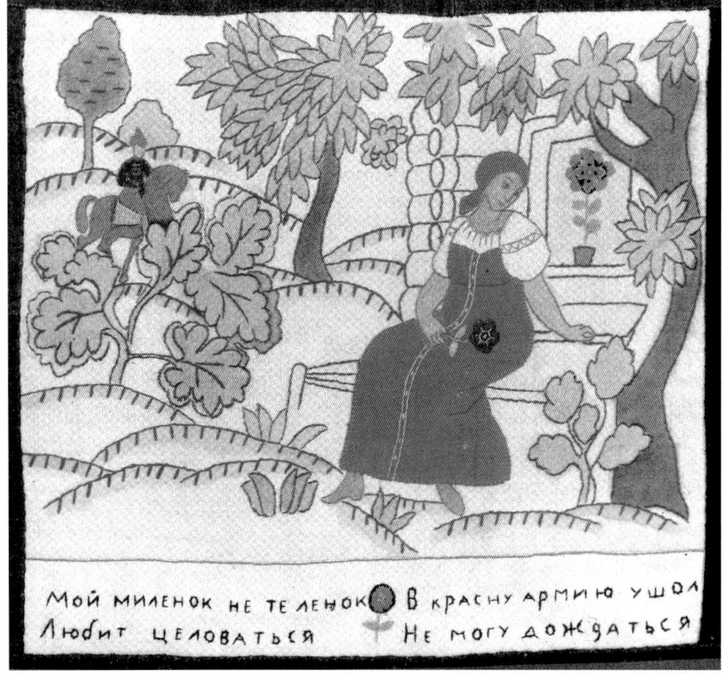

FIGURE 4

E. I. Lange, after a design by B. N. Lange, *chashtushki* (detail), embroidered panel, 1925. Photo: M. A. Nekrasova and S. M. Temerin, *Narodnye khudozhestvennye promysly* (Moscow, 1986), no. 219a. The inscription reads in part: "My sweetheart's no calf, he went to the Red Army, we had to kiss each other goodbye."

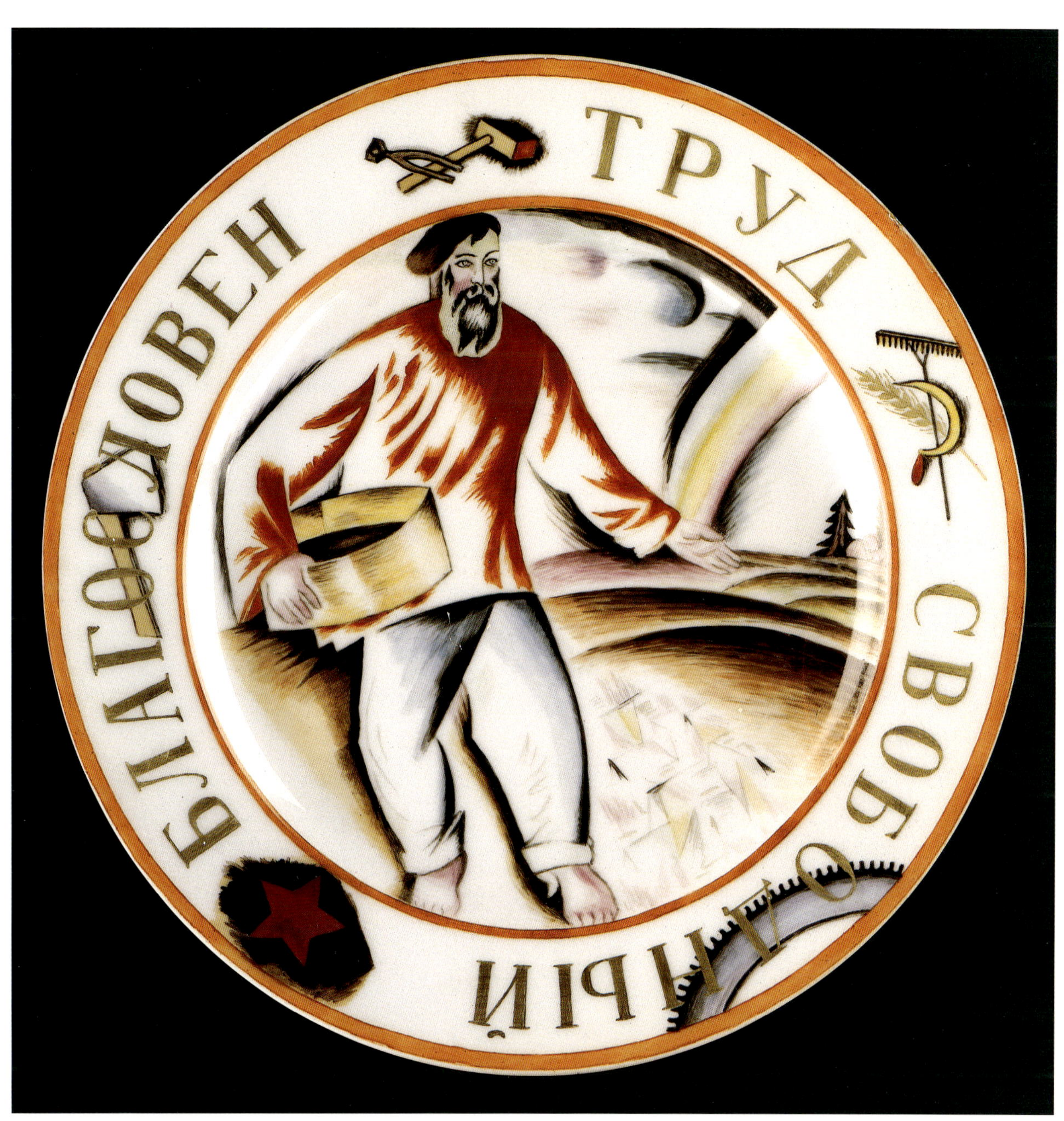

ТРУД
СВОБ
БЛАГОСЛОВЕН
ОДНЫЙ

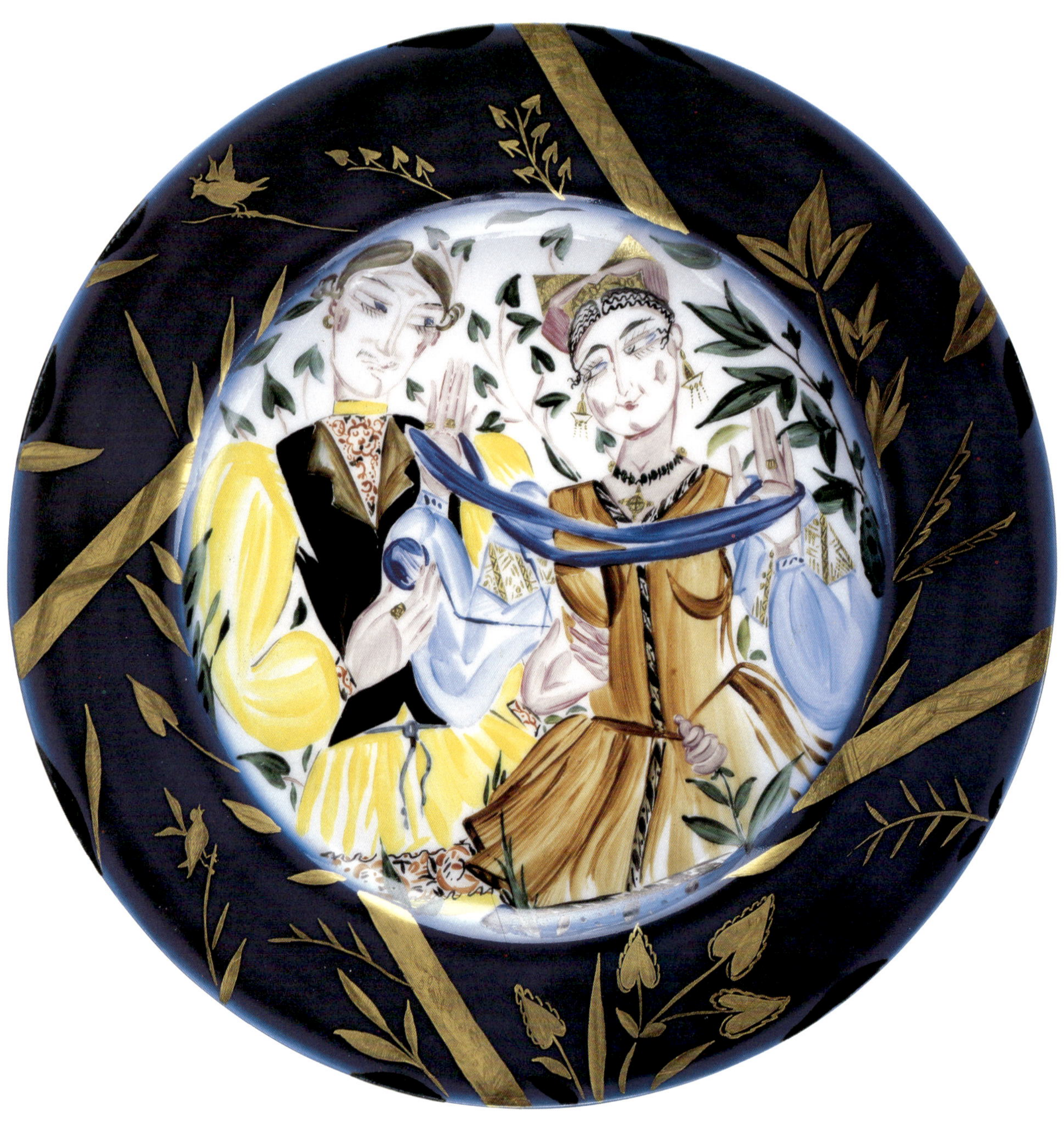

NO. 26
Aleksandra
Shchekotikhina-
Pototskaia
*Plate called "The Wool
Winders,"* 1921

ity and naturalness with which Soviet her-
aldry dovetailed with folk motifs and the
ease with which Chekhonin, Adamovich,
Shchekotikhina, and others could move
from images of peasants to commissars
and from saints to socialists verify the
underlying unity of Russian and Soviet
art. The linkage of traditional forms—the
imperial legacy as well as folk and popular culture—to new social and political
goals also reinforces the importance of the
commissions established in the first months
of the Revolution to preserve the monuments of the past.

Soviet porcelain aroused considerable
interest abroad. Participation in international exhibitions was essential to counter
accusations of artistic decline disseminated
in the anti-Soviet press; the quality of the
porcelain proved that this art, at least, had
not died out, but had developed along
new and vital lines.[22] At the 1925
International Exposition of Decorative and
Industrial Arts in Paris, the jury awarded
the State Porcelain Factory a large gold
medal for overall quality and gave individual medals to many designers of propaganda porcelain. Following another
exhibition in 1928, several French firms
offered to market Soviet porcelain in
Europe. In view of the growing visibility
abroad, the government export commission, Promeksport, urged artists to "devote
more attention to creating [works with]
national folk motifs."[23]

The artistic, commercial, and diplomat-
ic success of propaganda porcelain was
cause for celebration. But the high quality
and small volume of production left a siz-
able gap in fulfilling mass domestic needs
for practical but attractive utensils. In the
early 1930s, the State Academy of Art
History formed a commission to study the
"problems of the artistic formation of dishes for the masses," one of many commissions and conferences concerned with
the restructuring (perestroika) of daily life
under the New Economic Policy of 1922.[24]
The problem was not confined to porcelain, but it was especially obvious in this
field. Several ceramic firms in the Moscow
and Tver regions (in Dulevo, Verbiliki,
Konakovo, and other villages) took up the
slack in production; but without the partici-

pation of artists like Chekhonin, they relied
on old designs made for pre-Revolutionary,
"petit-bourgeois" tastes: nymphs, shepherds,
and "scènes galantes." Occasionally, a
painter might add a factory chimney to
a landscape or reclothe an elegant figure
as a Soviet peasant.[25] But the full-scale
restructuring of the applied arts envisioned
by artists and political leaders to create a
new environment for the people was never
realized, and genuine mass culture
remained a fiction. Propaganda porcelain
contributed little to the ideological and cultural education of Soviet citizens, most of
whom had to make do with leftovers from
the previous era or new products that were
admittedly second-rate—a situation that
has changed little to this day. From this
perspective, the artistic achievements of the
early Revolutionary years, the radical new
forms in applied arts, were only a shining
veneer over the cumbersome residue of a
backward culture.

It was in a luxury, court-art tradition
that the new government patrons placed
their enormous ambitions and considerable

Northern Dvina region,
Arkhangelsk province,
distaff (detail), painted
wood, first half of 19th
century. Photo: O.
Kruglova, *Russkaia nar-
odnaia rez'ba i rospis'
po derevu iz sobraniia
zagorskogo gosu-
darstvennogo istoriko-
khudozhestvennogo
muzeia-zapovednika*
(Moscow, 1974),
no. 71.

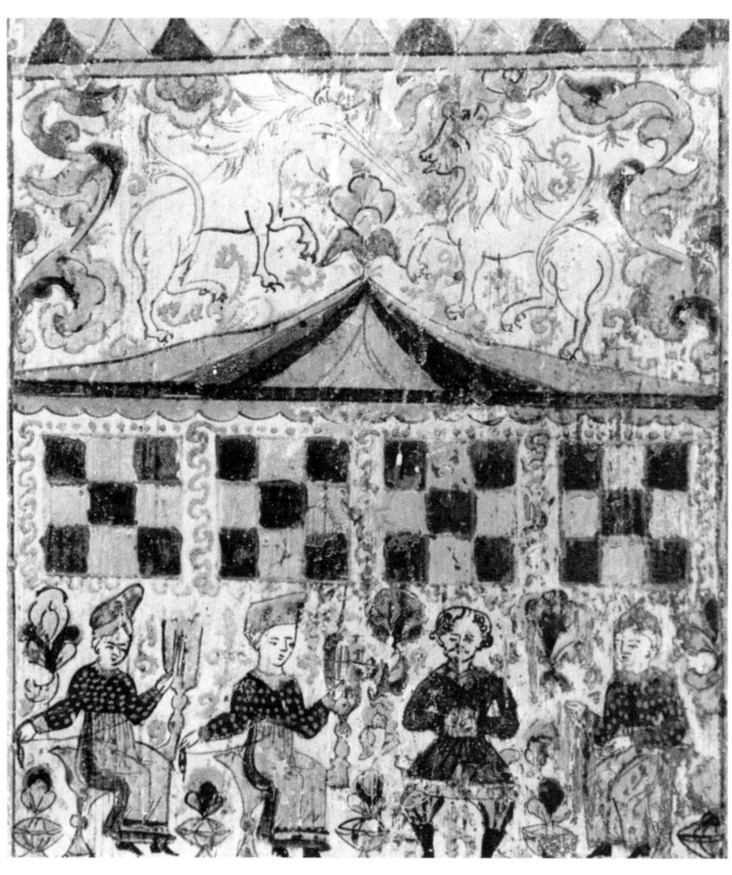

investment. Affirming continuity with the past and pointing toward the future, confirming a Russian heritage while embracing a Soviet identity and even reaching toward communist internationalism, propaganda porcelains served specific requirements of their own time and retained their fascination for future generations.

NOTES

1. See Richard Stites, "The Origins of Soviet Ritual Style: Symbol and Festival in the Russian Revolution," in Claes Arvidsson et al., *Symbols of Power* (Stockholm, 1987), pp. 23–42.
2. See Mikhail Guerman, *Art of the October Revolution* (Leningrad and New York, 1979), nos. 44, 82, 84.
3. Ibid., nos. 331, 337, 339.
4. See Wendy Ruth Salmond, "The Modernization of Folk Art in Russia: The Revival of the Kustar Art Industries, 1885–1917" (Ph.D. diss., Univ. of Texas at Austin, 1989), on Abramtsevo and later workshops. See Ol'ga Strugova, "The Decorative Art and Design of Russian *Moderne*," and Galina Smorodinova, "Russian Gold and Silver at the Turn of the Century," in *Twilight of the Tsars: Russian Art at the Turn of the Century,* exh. cat. Hayward Gallery, London (1991), pp. 223–28.
5. Illustrated in Marvin C. Ross, *Russian Porcelains* (Norman, Okla., 1968), pp. 312–20, 355–56, and plates.
6. See Vladimir Stasov, "Elena Dmitrievna Polenova," *Iskusstvo i khudzhestvennaia promyshlennost',* 1899, no. 13; Ivan Bilibin, "Narodnoe tvorchestvo russkogo severa," *Mir iskusstva,* 1904, no. 11.
7. Netta Peacock, "The New Movement in Russian Decorative Art" (*Studio,* 1901), repr. in *Twilight of the Tsars* (note 4), pp. 87–89.
8. Aleksandr Shevchenko, *Neoprimitivizm, ego teoriia, ego vozmozhnosti, ego dostizheniia (Neoprimitivism: Its Theory, Its Potentials, and Its Achievements)* (Moscow, 1913), trans. in John E. Bowlt, ed., *Russian Art of the Avant-Garde: Theory and Criticism, 1902–1934* (1976; rev. ed., New York, 1988), p. 45.
9. Natal'ia Goncharova, "Predislovie k katalogu vystavki" (Moscow, 1913), trans. as "Preface to Catalogue of One-Man Exhibition" in Bowlt (note 8), pp. 55–56.
10. Kazimir Malevich, "Fragments from 'Chapters from an Artist's Autobiography,' 1933," in *Kazimir Malevich 1878–1935,* exh. cat. The Armand Hammer

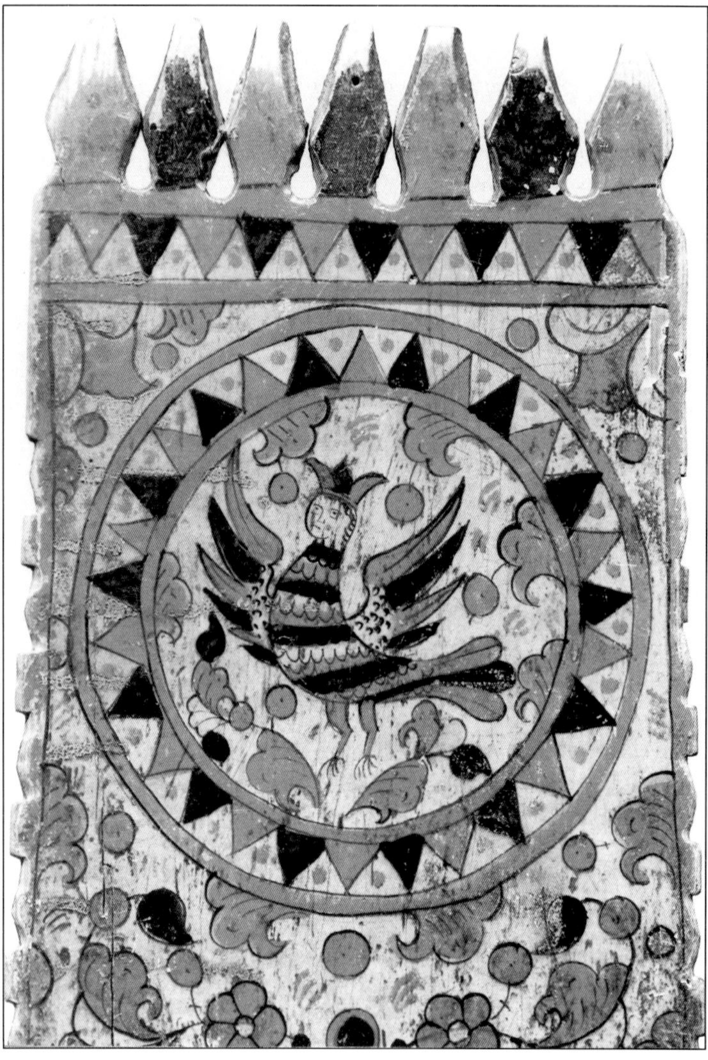

FIGURE 6
Northern Dvina region, Arkhangelsk province, *distaff* (detail showing *sirin*), painted wood, mid-19th century. Photo: Kruglova, no. 68.

Museum of Art and Cultural Center, Los Angeles (1990), pp. 174–75.

11. The 1919 decree "on measures affecting the folk arts industries" and related documents are reprinted in M. A. Nekrasova and S. M. Temerin, eds., *Narodnye khudozhestvennye promysly 1917–1932* (Moscow, 1986), vol. 1, pp. 19–20, 35–39, 111–15, 206–207. For a discussion of Soviet direction of applied arts, see B. N. Alekseev, "Khudozhestvennaia promyshlennost' (1917–1920)," and S. M. Temerin, "Khudozhestvennaia promyshlennost' (1921–1934)," in I. E. Grabar', V. S. Kemenov, and V. N. Lazarev, eds., *Istoriia russkogo iskusstva* (Moscow, 1957), vol. 11, pp. 156–66, 559–73.

12. Aleksandr Saltykov, *Russkaia narodnaia keramika* (Moscow, 1960), pp. 19–20.

13. See Ol'ga S. Popova, *Russkaia narodnaia kerami-ka. Gzhel', Skopin, Dymkovo* (Moscow, 1957); for greater detail and illustrations, see T. Dul'kina and N. Grigor'evna, *Gzhel'. Keramika 18–19 vekov. Keramika 20 veka* (Moscow, 1983) and *Keramika Gzheli* (Moscow, 1988).

14. Dul'kina and Grigor'evna (note 13, 1988), pp. 127–29.

15. Nekrasova and Temerin (note 11), vol. 2, gives examples in several media. The philosophy behind this process appears in A. B. Saltykov, *Ispol'zovanie narodnykh traditsii v razvitii sovetskogo prikladnogo iskusstva* (Moscow, 1956). For other aspects see the chapter "Reshaping Folk Art in the Soviet Era" in Alison Hilton, *Russian Folk Art and the Patterns of Life* (Bloomington, Ind., 1992).

16. See Ol'ga V. Kruglova, *Narodnaia rospis' severnoi Dviny* (Moscow, 1987).

17. The styles of northern Russian folk arts and their relationship to social customs are discussed in Hilton (note 15).

18. *Sovetskii kalendar* (Moscow, 1919), illustrated in *Graphica Russa 1917/1930,* exh. cat. Palazzo Strozzi, Florence (1992), no. 96. The artist is not identified.

19. Roerich designed a mosaic of the mounted Archangel Michael for a church in 1906, illustrated in E. Poliakova, *Rerikh* (Moscow, 1973). Goncharova used this icon type as a model for a lithograph of the Archangel Michael in her series *Mystical Images of War,* made at the beginning of World War I; see Alison Hilton, "Natalia Goncharova and the Iconography of Revelation," *Studies in Iconography* 13 (Fall 1991), pp. 232–57. Bilibin created many variants of the mounted *bogatyr* figure in illustrations and stage designs throughout his career; see Sergei Golynets, *Ivan Bilibin* (Leningrad and London, 1981).

20. A. K. Lansere, *Sovetskii farfor. Iskusstvo Leningradskogo gosudarstvennogo farforogo zavoda imeni M. V. Lomonosova / Soviet Porcelain: Art of the M. V. Lomonosov State Porcelain Factory, Leningrad* (Leningrad, 1974), pl. 12.

21. Alekseev (note 11), p. 164.

22. Temerin (note 11), pp. 569–70.

23. Ibid., p. 570.

24. Ibid., pp. 571–72.

25. Ibid., p. 571.

Catalogue Entries

Objects are listed alphabetically by designer. Dates indicate the year of painting.

NUMBER 1

**Mikhail Mikhailovich Adamovich
Plate, 1921**

This plate commemorates the Third International, or Comintern, formed in Moscow in 1919. It was a Soviet-dominated, international organization of communist working people's groups whose mission was to spread revolution. It was believed that the communist government in Russia had a better chance of surviving if it had a network of politically sympathetic allies for trade and defense. The center is decorated with a segmented, multicolored inscription reading "Da Zdravstvuet 3 Internatsional" (Long live the Third International). The number three has been decorated with flowers, and the entire inscription floats above a skyline of factories and smokestacks.

Underside: Imperial Porcelain Factory mark of Alexander III dated [18]93; State Porcelain Factory mark dated 1921; "Po ris. khudozh. Adamovicha" (From a design by the artist Adamovich); initials A. R. V. for an unidentified factory painter.

Diam.: 9⅛ in. (23.2 cm)
Illustrated p. 39

Similar objects are illustrated or discussed in: *Art into Production*, p. 37 (with inscription in German).

NUMBER 2 A-B

**Mikhail Mikhailovich Adamovich
Cup and saucer called "Lenin with Red Star," 1921**

The cup is decorated with images that symbolize the social changes that took place in Russia after the Revolution. A globe stands next to a red star that contains the hammer and plow of the Red Army. Red Army men in the latest uniform design march four abreast toward a factory. Next to them is a portrait of Lenin (based on the eighth plate of Natan Al'tman's 1920 album *Lenin, Drawings*) and the initials R.S.F.S.R. above him. A stylized rendering of the date of the Revolution ("X/25/1917") and a hammer and sickle are stretched across the plate. The saucer uses a sparser arrangement of the decorative elements on the cup, minus the portrait of Lenin, the globe, and the factory.

Underside (cup): Undated Imperial Porcelain Factory mark of Alexander III, numbered 744894; State Porcelain Factory mark dated 1922, numbered 3/21.
Underside (saucer): Imperial Porcelain Factory mark of Alexander III dated [18]89; State Porcelain Factory mark dated 1921, numbered 3/21.

Height (cup): 2¾ in. (7 cm)
Diam. (saucer): 6¼ in. (15.9 cm)
Illustrated p. 31

This cup and saucer appear in Lobanov-Rostovsky, 1990, pl. 6. Similar objects are illustrated or discussed in: Atterbury, 1986, p. 57; *Avanguardia Russa*, p. 155 (incorrectly attributed to Natan Al'tman); Tolstoi, 1989, p. 174 (incorrectly attributed to Natan Al'tman).

NUMBER 3

**Mikhail Mikhailovich Adamovich
Plate, 1921**

The center is decorated with a stylized hammer and sickle, both painted with a green and red floral pattern, and the date "25 Oktiabria 1917 goda." The border is decorated with the German phrase "Es lebe die 3. Internationale!" (Long live the Third International!).

Underside: Imperial Porcelain Factory mark of Nicholas II dated 1905; State Porcelain Factory mark dated 1921.

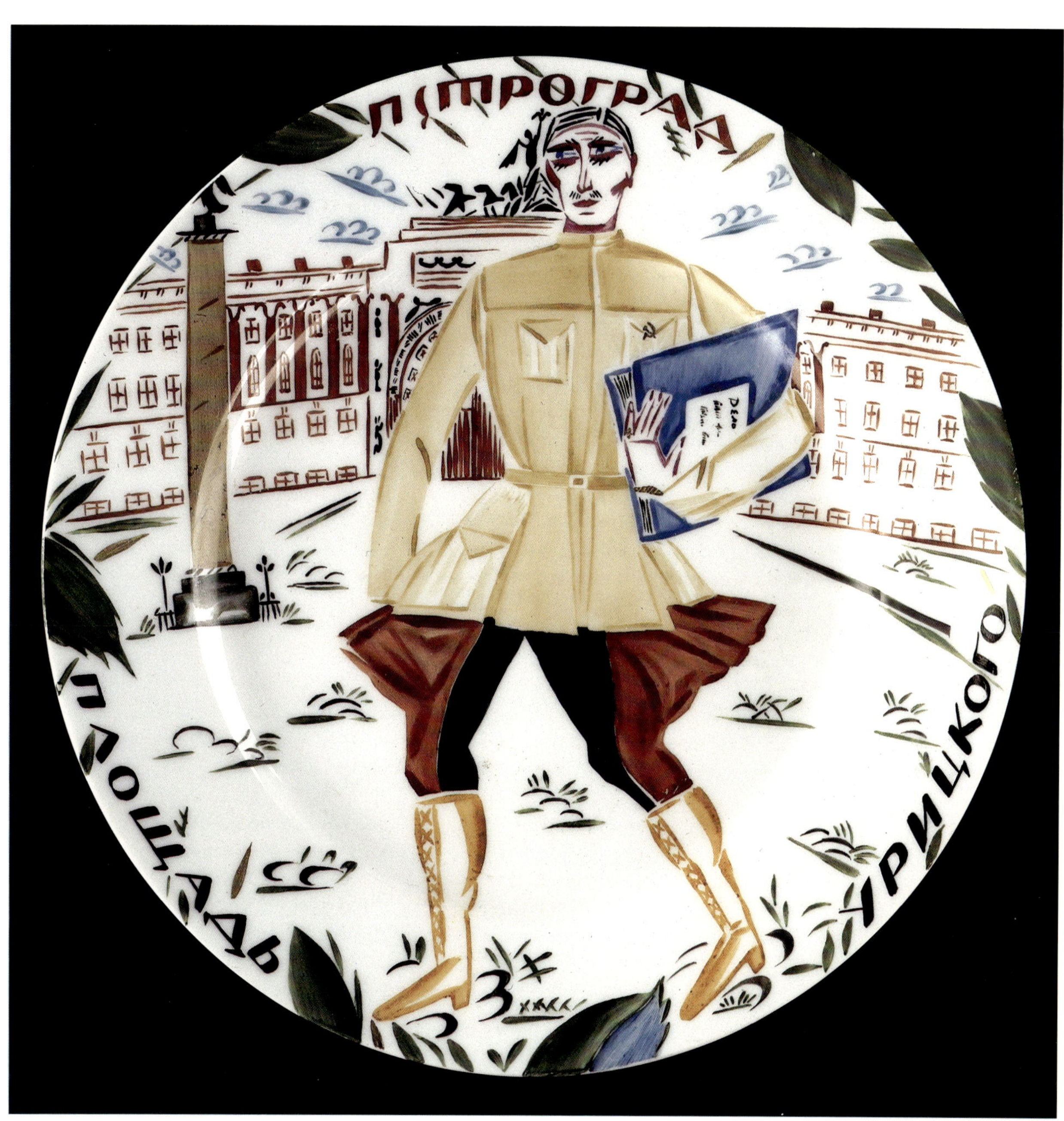

NO. 28
Aleksandra
Shchekotikhina-
Pototskaia
Plate called "The
Commissar," 1922

Diam.: 9¾ in. (24.8 cm)
Illustrated p. 59

Similar objects are illustrated or discussed in:
Christie's, Oct. 6, 1988, lot 282, and Oct. 10,
1990, lot 310; Lansere, 1974, pl. 4; Lobanov-
Rostovsky, 1990, pl. 10.

NUMBER 4

Mikhail Mikhailovich Adamovich
Plate, 1922

The inscription on this plate reads "Kto ne rabo-
taet, tot ne est" (He who does not work, does
not eat). The phrase, which paraphrases Saint
Paul (2 Thess. 3:10) and was often used in propaganda posters, was written into the first
Soviet Constitution of 1918. The proverb is illustrated quite literally by a supplementary ration
card on top of a worker's identification card.
A sheet with a bust of Lenin, a red star with a
hammer and sickle, and the initials R.S.F.S.R.
crush the Russian imperial eagle.

Underside: Imperial Porcelain Factory mark of
Nicholas II dated 1902; State Porcelain Factory
mark dated 1922, numbered 243/7.

Diam.: 10⅜ in. (26.4 cm)
Illustrated on cover and p. 87

Similar objects are illustrated or discussed in:
Andreeva, 1971, p. 142, and 1975, p. 179;
*Art Born of the October Revolution; Art into
Production*, p. 37; Atterbury, 1986, p. 57;
Baranova, 1983, pl. 130; Christie's, April
23, 1991, lot 69; Guerman, 1979, pl. 260;
Lobanov-Rostovsky, 1990, pp. 32-33; Makarov,
1984, p. 52.

NUMBER 5

Mikhail Mikhailovich Adamovich
Plate called "The Red Star," 1922

Early Soviet porcelain acclaimed the expressly
political, ideological basis of the new country—
a dictatorship of the workers and peasants—
and the industrial aspirations of the relatively
underdeveloped nation by utilizing working
tools as symbolic and decorative elements. The

cobalt blue background of the rim of this plate
has been decorated with agricultural and industrial tools in gilding: wheat sheaves and sickle,
aerator, scythe, rake, hammer and nails, saw
blade, cog and spring, triangle and compass,
and a fish in a net. The reserve contains a hammer and plow, symbol of the worker/peasant
army, within a red star, and the initials
R.S.F.S.R. in gold floral lettering.

Underside: Imperial Porcelain Factory mark of
Nicholas II dated 1902; State Porcelain Factory
mark dated 1922, numbered 216/3.

Diam.: 9¼ in. (23.5 cm)
Illustrated p. 15

Similar objects are illustrated or discussed
in: Alekseev, 1962, p. 21; *Art into Production*,
p. 37; Baranova, 1983, pl. 128; Christie's,
Oct. 5, 1989, lot 347; Gollerbach, 1922,
p. 9; *Das Leben zur Kunst Machen*, p. 90;
Lobanov-Rostovsky, 1990, pl. 66; de
Tiesenhausen, 1989, pp. 82-84; Tolstoi,
1989, p. 187.

NUMBER 6

Mikhail Mikhailovich Adamovich
**Plate called "The Fifth Anniversary of the Red
Army," 1923**

A Red Army soldier strides across a map of
the Soviet Union wearing the new uniform
designed by Boris Kustodiev, whose *Budenny*
cap and gray greatcoat had won the government's 1918–19 contest; Tolstoi (1989, pp.
263, 296-97) reports that their shape was taken
from old Russian caftans and helmets.
The soldier bayonets torn yellow flags marked
with the names of the White generals and
admirals Kolchak, Iudenich, Vrangel',
Diederikhs, and Denikin. British, American,
Japanese, and Polish flags, representing the
Allied forces that had blockaded the early
Bolshevik republic, lie among the flags of the
Whites. The plate resembles Dmitri S. Moor's
1920/21 poster *Be On Guard* (repr. in White,
1988, p. 90) in which a giant Red Army man
with the face of Leon Trotsky, architect of the
army and first Commissar of War, defends the
western border of Russia from the threat of inva-
sion by the Poles. This plate was extensively

repainted after the repair of a break. During repainting, the gold border was inscribed incorrectly "D[a] Zdravstvu[et] Krasnaia Armiia, 1918–1923" (Long live the Red Army). X-rays show the properly spelled inscription below the new paint.

Underside: The original marks were also mistranscribed during repainting. No factory marks, numbered 129/345, mistakenly dated 1921 (two years prior to the fifth anniversary); "Po ris. Adamovicha" (From a design by Adamovich), initial V. for an unidentified factory painter.

Diam.: 16¾ in. (42.6 cm)
Illustrated p. 10

Similar objects are illustrated or discussed in: Andreeva, 1975, p. 178; Lansere, 1974, pl. 5; Lobanov-Rostovsky, 1990, pl. 4; Makarov, 1984, p. 51.

NUMBER 7

Natan Isaevich Al'tman
Plate, 1921, prototype 1919

The border of this plate is decorated with the slogan "Zemlia trudiashchimsia" (Land to the workers) in red lettering. Against the solid green background, the center contains an image in red of several factories cradled by a crossed hammer and sickle within a diamond-shaped border. The emblem was copied from Al'tman's design for the decoration of the General Staff Building in Petrograd (see Kettering, "Introduction," fig. 1), where the Provisional Government had made its last stand, on the first anniversary of the October Revolution. A banner hung in the building's central arch carried Al'tman's design and the inscription "Petrograd workers' commune." Al'tman is reported to have chosen red and green to represent the workers and the peasants of communist Russia. Nina Lobanov-Rostovsky has noted that the green hue of this plate differs from others made in this year. It is possible that it is a later, authorized copy made for exhibition abroad.

Underside: Imperial Porcelain Factory mark of Nicholas II dated 1896; State Porcelain Factory mark dated 1921.

Diam.: 9½ in. (24.1 cm)

Illustrated p. 9

Similar objects are illustrated or discussed in: Andreeva, 1975, p. 149; *Art Born of the October Revolution; Art into Production*, p. 42; Gollerbakh and Farmakovskii, 1924, p. 120; Lansere, 1974, pl. 4; Lobanov-Rostovsky, 1990, pl. 11; Makarov, 1984, p. 53; *La Rivoluzione in salotto*, pl. 1; Sotheby's, Nov. 30, 1990, lot 198; Tolstoi, 1980, pl. 25, and 1989, p. 185.

NUMBER 8

Veniamin Pavlovich Belkin
Plate called "The Sower," 1920

The border is inscribed with the phrase "Blagosloven trud svobodnyi" (Blessed is free labor), tools of agricultural and industrial labor (an axe, pliers and hammer, sickle and rake, and gear), and a red star. In the center, a rainbow in black, yellow, and pink appears beyond a barefoot, bearded man in peasant dress who sows seed in a newly plowed field at the edge of a pine forest.

Underside: Imperial Porcelain Factory mark dated 1913 (or 1915); State Porcelain Factory mark dated 1920; initials M. K. for factory painter Maria Petrovna Kirilova.

Diam.: 9¼ in. (23.5 cm)
Illustrated p. 61

Similar objects are illustrated or discussed in: Andreeva, 1975, p. 153; *Art into Production*, p. 42; Gollerbach, 1922, p. 14; Guerman, 1979, p. 355; Lansere, 1974, pl. 29.

NUMBER 9

Sergei Vasil'evich Chekhonin
Plate, 1922, prototype 1918

The center is decorated with the State Porcelain Factory emblem—a hammer, a sickle, and a section of a gear—in gold against a small black disk. Fruit and flowers surround the motif.

Underside: Imperial Porcelain Factory mark of Nicholas II dated 1898; State Porcelain Factory mark dated 1922, numbered 424.10;

signed V. Freze by the factory painter Varvara Petrovna Freze.

Diam.: 9¾ in. (24.8 cm)
Illustrated p. 57

Similar objects are illustrated or discussed in: Andreeva, 1971, p. 136, and 1975, p. 133; *Art into Production,* p. 26; Kogan, 1925, p. 185; Lansere, 1974, pl. 5; Lobanov-Rostovsky, 1990, pl. 68; Lukomski, 1925, p. 205; Tolstoi, 1980, pl. 10, and 1989, p. 171 (the caption incorrectly identifies it as a version of Vil'de's "Victory to the workers of the 25th of October" [see cat. no. 40]).

NUMBER 10

**Sergei Vasil'evich Chekhonin
Plate, 1920**

In the arc segments demarked by the points of a red star, the sentence reads "Tsarstvu rabochikh i krest'ian ne budet kontsa" (The kingdom of the workers and peasants will never end). The center (within the red star) shows a bright sun of blank white porcelain rising above the word "Kommuna" (Commune). A rough hammer constructed of an unfinished stone and branch and a serrated sickle lie at the base. The inscription on this plate is an example of the ideological mistakes often made by artists participating in propaganda work in the period after the Revolution. Lenin criticized a poster with the same prophecy because it indicated that the classless society of true socialism, the ultimate goal of the Bolshevik revolution, would never be attained (see White, 1988, p. 115).

Underside: Imperial Porcelain Factory mark of Nicholas II dated 1898; State Porcelain Factory mark dated 1920.

Diam.: 9⁷⁄₁₆ in. (24 cm)
Illustrated p. 13

Similar objects are illustrated or discussed in: Efros and Punin, 1924, p. 105; Lobanov-Rostovsky, 1990, pl. 13.

**Sergei Vasil'evich Chekhonin
Plate, 1922, prototype 1920**

The center is decorated with the phrase "Tsarstvu rabochikh i krest'ian ne budet kontsa" (The kingdom of the workers and peasants will never end). This plate resembles another plate by Chekhonin (cat. no. 10) that bears the same inscription and sun, here marked by the initials R.S.F.S.R. rising above a hammer and sickle in the molding and on the edge of the rim.

Underside: Imperial Porcelain Factory mark of Nicholas II dated 1913; State Porcelain Factory five-year anniversary mark dated 1922; "1. 10" (an atypical numbering system).

Diam.: 12½ in. (31.8 cm)
Illustrated p. 41

This plate appears in Lobanov-Rostovsky, 1990, pl. 15. Similar objects are illustrated or discussed in: Andreeva, 1971, p. 133, and 1975, p. 139; *Art into Production,* p. 23; Guerman, p. 352; Tolstoi, 1980, p. 10, and 1989, p. 162.

NUMBER 12

**Sergei Vasil'evich Chekhonin
Plate called "Cubist Design with Hammer and Sickle," 1921**

Many artists felt that the radical change in government structure should be accompanied by a similar restructuring in artistic styles and institutions. By utilizing geometric forms that he identified as "Cubist," Chekhonin associates the revolutionary character of the government with a revolutionary style in art that was viewed, both positively and negatively, as having disrupted and rejected classical pictorial and representational systems. The border is decorated with an incised gilt pattern and bright geometric shapes. A hammer and sickle and a section of a gear are rendered in red, black, and gold in the reserve.

Underside: Obliterated mark; State Porcelain Factory mark dated 1921.

Diam.: 9½ in. (24.1 cm)

Illustrated p. 38

Similar objects are discussed or illustrated in
Art Born of the October Revolution; Lansere,
1974, pl. 29; *Das Leben zur Kunst Machen,* pl.
30; Lobanov-Rostovsky, 1990, pl. 67; *Paris-
Moscou;* Tolstoi, 1989, p. 189.

NUMBER 13

Sergei Vasil'evich Chekhonin
Plate, 1921

Celebrating the anniversary of the Revolution,
the center is inscribed "1917 1921 4 goda"
(four years) in orange and black lettering.
The edge of the molding is covered by a black
band with a white floral and leaf pattern. A red
ribbon, much like that of Chekhonin's famous
1919 "Red Ribbon" plate, is painted around the
edge of the border (see Lobanov-Rostovsky,
1990, pl. 69).

Underside: Canceled, obliterated mark; canceled State Porcelain Factory mark dated 1921.

Diam.: 10 in. (25.4 cm)
Illustrated p. 25

NUMBER 14 A–C

Sergei Vasil'evich Chekhonin
Milk jug, teapot, hot-water jug, after 1934,
prototype 1922

The tea set is decorated with the floral and foli-
ated initials R.S.F.S.R. (Russian Soviet Federal
Socialist Republic) and crossed hammers and
sickles. The back of the teapot also includes
wheat sheaves against a red ribbon. Matching
plates (not in the Tuber Collection) are more pro-
fusely decorated than the teapot and jugs. Black
blossoms, resembling those in the letter F of
R.S.F.S.R., embellish the area around the initials,
and the borders are adorned with a design of
foliage and gold flowers.

Underside (milk jug): Undated State Porcelain
Factory mark.
Underside (teapot): State Porcelain Factory mark
dated 1926, illegible initials of a
factory painter.

Underside (hot-water jug): State Porcelain
Factory mark dated 1934 or 1936.
Height (milk jug): 5¼ in. (13.3 cm)
Height (teapot): 7 in. (17.8 cm)
Diam. (lid): 2⅜ in. (6 cm)
Height (hot-water jug): 5⅛ in. (13 cm)
Illustrated p. 24

The tea set is unpublished. Illustrations of similar
plates, possibly from the service, appear
in: Andreeva, 1971, p. 138, and 1975,
p. 145; Efros and Punin, 1924, p. 6; Guerman,
1979, p. 356; Kogan, 1925, p. 187; Lansere,
1974, pl. 2; Makarov, 1984, p. 47; Tolstoi,
1989, p. 167; "Tschechonin," 1929,
pp. 221–24.

NUMBER 15

Liubov' Nikolaevna Gaush
Plate, 1921

Stylized black letters constructed of gold-han-
dled sickles and gold-headed hammers form the
word "Rossiia" (Russia) among profuse foliage.
The blank central circle may indicate that the
plate was unfinished.

Underside: Imperial Porcelain Factory mark of
Nicholas II dated 1906; State Porcelain Factory
mark dated 1921; initials L. G.

Diam.: 14¼ in. (36.2 cm)
Illustrated p. 56

Similar objects are illustrated or discussed in:
Christie's, Apr. 27, 1990, lot 333.

NUMBER 16

Alisa Rudol'fovna Golenkina
Plate, 1920

The design for this large plate seems to be
based on nineteenth-century funerary or memori-
al art, in which flowers and plants sprout anew
from desolate, rocky landscapes. A disheveled
man, whose appearance suggests that he may
be a Parisian communard, rather than a veteran
of the Russian Revolution, holds a banner reading "Luchshii pamiatnik pogibshim brat'iam—
pobeda kommunizma" (The best monument to

[our] fallen brothers is the victory of communism). The ghostlike, black and white figure stands next to a small hill with pink flowers under a cloudy, slate-blue sky. Factories with smokestacks are visible in the background. This plate, like Vladimir I. Kozlinskii's poster (repr. in White, 1988, p. 87) "Mertvetsy Parizhskoi Kommuny voskresli pod krasnym znamenem Sovetov!" (The dead of the Paris Commune have risen again under the red banner of the Soviets!), recalls the victims of failed socialist revolutions in Europe. It suggests that rather than mourn the dead—of the Revolution, the Paris Commune, or the short-lived soviet republics in Germany—and the trials of life in the new society, citizens should contribute to the creation of communism, here represented by industrial development.

Underside: Partially obliterated Imperial Porcelain Factory mark of Alexander III; State Porcelain Factory mark dated 1920; initials A.G.

Diam.: 13¾ in. (34.9 cm)
Illustrated p. 54

This plate appears in Christie's, Apr. 24, 1991, lot 70.

NUMBER 17

Alisa Rudol'fovna Golenkina
Plate called "The Red Genius," 1922

A winged horse and its rider carrying a torch fly above burning classical ruins. Rays of light pour forth from behind clouds of smoke. The border is decorated with the German slogan "Wir Entflammen die Ganze Welt mit dem Feuer der III. Internationale" (We inflame the entire world with the fire of the Third International). Many propaganda plates carry German inscriptions because the Third International was particularly interested in Germany, whose postwar political and economic situation made it the most plausible location for the next communist revolution. The world of the past and its economic and social systems are represented by the ruins of classical architecture. The destruction of a classical building in a fiery explosion was often used to represent cultural changes brought on by the Revolution.

The image for this plate was taken from a 1919 Soviet calendar published in Moscow; it had been recycled for a 1920 literacy poster, the rider carrying an open book, with the caption "Literacy is the path to communism" (repr. in White, 1988, p. 111).

Underside: Imperial Porcelain Factory mark of Alexander III dated [18]92; State Porcelain Factory mark dated 1922, numbered 431/1; signed V. Freze by the factory painter Varvara Petrovna Freze.

Diam.: 9⅝ in. (24.5 cm)
Illustrated p. 35

This plate appears in Christie's, Apr. 27, 1990, lot 331. Similar objects are illustrated or discussed in: Alekseev, 1962, pp. 104–105; Lansere, 1974, pl. 4; Lobanov-Rostovsky, 1989, p. 137, and 1990, pl. 25; *La Rivoluzione in salotto*, p. 36; Sotheby's, Nov. 30, 1990, lot 185; Tolstoi, 1989, p. 195.

NUMBER 18

Zinaida Viktorovna Kobyletskaia
Plate, 1921

During both the 1905 and 1917 revolutions in Russia, workers formed democratic councils called soviets, whose members elected representatives to voice the workers' needs and opinions to factory management and the government. The word *sovet*, meaning council, is derived from the Russian verb *sovetovat'*, to advise. In 1917, when Vladimir Lenin returned to Russia from exile, he delivered a speech known as his "April Theses," in which he cited the workers' and soldiers' soviets as the key to a revolutionary transformation of the Russian government. He summarized his view with the slogan "All power to the soviets," which became a rallying cry for the Revolution of October 25. The rim is painted with the message "Da Zdravstvuet vlast' sovetov! 1921" (Long live the power of the soviets!). Blue storm clouds roil around a vibrant red star composed of flames and emitting lightning bolts.

Underside: State Porcelain Factory mark dated 1921; "Po ris. khud. Kobyletskoi" (From a design by the artist Kobyletskaia); initials N. G.

for factory painter Natal'ia Girshfeld.

Diam.: 12 in. (30.5 cm)
Illustrated p. 42

Similar objects are illustrated or discussed in:
Atterbury, 1986, p. 57; Lobanov-Rostovsky,
1990, pl. 29.

NUMBER 19

Zinaida Viktorovna Kobyletskaia
Plate, 1921

The Russian phrase "Da Zdravstvuet VIII S'ezd
Sovetov" (Long live the Eighth Congress of
the Soviets) dominates this plate, with the
word "soviets" in bold red lettering in the
center. The beginning of the phrase, with
incised gold leaves, wheat, and an acorn,
decorates the border.

Underside: Imperial Porcelain Factory mark of
Nicholas II dated 1898; State Porcelain Factory
mark dated 1921.

Diam.: 9¾ in. (24.8 cm)
Illustrated p. 91

This plate appears in Christie's, Apr. 24, 1991,
lot 67. A similar one is in Tolstoi, 1989, p. 192.

NUMBER 20

Vladimir Vasil'evich Lebedev
Plate called "Pravda," undated

The letters of the word "Truth" lie in one section
of the center. The design is contiguous across
the center and rim, the whole painted black
and brown with dark green and red areas
in a fractured style resembling Lebedev's
Cubo-Futurist paintings of the period.
Abstracted, gilt forms represent a sickle
and wheat stalks.

Underside: Imperial Porcelain Factory mark of
Nicholas II dated 1910; undated State Porcelain
Factory mark numbered 174(?); "Po ris. V.
Lebedeva" (From a design by V. Lebedev).

Diam.: 9½ in. (24.1 cm)

Illustrated p. 45

Similar objects are illustrated or discussed in:
Abramova, 1927, following p. 22; Christie's,
Apr. 27, 1990, lot 330, and Oct. 10, 1990,
lot 309; Franzke, 1977, p. 202.

NUMBER 21

Elizaveta Berngardovna Rozendorf
or Rudol'f Fedorovich Vil'de
Plate, 1920

The Russian phrase "Da Zdravstvuet VIII
S'ezd Sovetov—1920" (Long live the Eighth
Congress of the Soviets) is inscribed on the border. The reserve is decorated with a
hammer and sickle and two wheat sheaves
encircling a red star. The Eighth Congress
of the Soviets was the eighth Communist Party
conference, held in March 1919. At the
Congress a system of supreme party entities
was introduced, and the R.S.F.S.R. officially
joined the Third International.

Underside: Obliterated mark; State Porcelain
Factory mark dated 1920.

Diam.: 9½ in. (24.1 cm)
Illustrated p. 40

Similar objects are illustrated or discussed in:
Art into Production, p. 43; *Avanguardia Russa*,
p. 159.

NUMBER 22

Elizaveta Bergardovna Rozendorf
Plate, 1920

The reserve of this plate is decorated with black
and white Cyrillic initials for R.S.F.S.R rendered
partially by flowers. Idyllic scenes of a prosperous
countryside cover the border: well-spaced, single-
family homes in good repair stand next to wells,
sheds, and pine trees. The famine in the Volga
region was not widely known until the summer of
1921. Because the majority of these plates were
distributed in urban centers, a plate such as this
would have reassured viewers that the countryside
was prosperous and would continue to meet the
needs of urban consumers. The juxtaposition of a

sound and stable countryside with the initials of
the Soviet state suggested that rural prosperity had
been achieved under the new government.

Underside: State Porcelain Factory mark
dated 1920.

Diam.: 8½ in. (21.6 cm)
Illustrated p. 6

Similar objects are illustrated or discussed in:
Christie's, Apr. 24, 1991, lot 66; Sysoeva,
1989, p. 164.

NUMBER 23

**Aleksandra Vasil'evna Shchekotikhina-Pototskaia
Cup and saucer, 1919**

Considering Shchekotikhina-Pototskaia's interest
in Russian peasant culture, this cup probably represents a scene from a folktale. A young blond
man wearing a heavy brown coat with decorative lacings and patterned pants is barely able to
stay in the saddle of the horse he is riding. He
falls backward, grabbing for his cap and the
horse's reins. The animal's legs are held straight
in front of its body as it jumps across a river. The
rocks, vines, flowers, and sun at the edge of the
river are all rendered in gilt against a plain
white background. The remainder of the surface
of the cup and the entire surface of the saucer
are painted with heavy green leaves and large
flowers against a sky-blue background. A few
gilt clouds and stars are painted on the saucer.

Underside (cup): Obliterated mark; State
Porcelain Factory mark dated 1919; abbrevia-
tion "Shchek."
Underside (saucer): Obliterated mark; State
Porcelain Factory mark dated 1919; initial "Shch."

Height (cup): 2⅝ in. (6.7 cm)
Diam. (saucer): 5⅝ in. (14.3 cm)
Illustrated p. 52

NUMBER 24

**Aleksandra Vasil'evna Shchekotikhina-Pototskaia
Plate called "Angel and Baby," 1920**

All previously published examples of this design

have been painted on rectangular platters. In this
image, an angel wearing a patterned robe cradles a tightly swaddled baby in its arms as it flies
above a village. The roofs of small houses, the
steeple of a church, the moon, stars, and clouds
fill the space in the background. Shchekotikhina-
Pototskaia's signature is visible above the decorative border in the lower left. The style and subject
of this plate can be traced to the artist's interest in
traditional motifs and themes of Russian folk art.

Underside: State Porcelain Factory mark dated
1920; "Shchek."; "no. 237."

Diam.: 13 in. (33 cm)
Illustrated p. 51

Platters similar to this are illustrated or discussed
in: Andreeva, 1975, p. 156; Lansere, 1974,
pl. 12.

NUMBER 25

**Aleksandra Vasil'evna Shchekotikhina-Pototskaia
Plate called "The Sailor Takes a Walk," 1921**

The inscription reads "1 Maia 1921g. gorod
Petrograd" (May 1, 1921, City of Petrograd).
A sailor, in a *Baltflot* (Baltic Fleet) cap and uniform, walks arm in arm along an embankment
with a woman dressed in a headscarf, short
skirt, and boots. The sailor, perhaps on leave for
May Day, appears to have a hammer and sickle
tattooed on his sternum. Behind them, sailboats
are visible on the Neva.

Underside: Imperial Porcelain Factory mark of
Nicholas II dated 1905; State Porcelain Factory
mark dated 1921; "Po ris. Shchekatikhinoi"
(From a design by Shchekotikhina); initials
M. K. for the factory painter Maria Petrovna
Kirilova.

Diam.: 9⅞ in. (25.2 cm)
Illustrated p. 22

Similar objects are illustrated or discussed in:
Andreeva, 1975, p. 166; Christie's, Apr. 26,
1989, lot 256; Guerman, 1979, p. 348;
Makarov, 1984, p. 55; Lobanov-Rostovsky,
1990, pl. 37.

**Aleksandra Vasil'evna Shchekotikhina-Pototskaia
Plate called "The Wool Winders," 1921**

A peasant couple winds wool against a background of green and gilt leaves. The blue-eyed, mustachioed man, dressed in a yellow shirt and black waistcoat, winds the ball of blue wool. The woman, wear-ing a blue shirt, a brown *sarafan* and a *kokoshnik* (a headdress resembling a crown), returns the man's gaze as she winds the skein.

Underside: Obliterated mark, State Porcelain Factory mark dated 1921; "Po ris. A. V. Shchekotikhinoi" (From a design by A. V. Shchekotikhina); initials M. K. for factory painter Maria Petrovna Kirilova.

Diam.: 9½ in. (24.1 cm)
Illustrated p. 62

Similar objects are illustrated or discussed in: Christie's, Apr. 24, 1991, lot 68; Noskovich, 1959, p. 11.

**Aleksandra Vasil'evna Shchekotikhina-Pototskaia
Plate, 1921**

This design is based on Shchekotikhina-Pototskaia's "Bell Ringer" plate, created in honor of the Eighth Congress of the Soviets in 1920–21. This bell ringer is considerably older, and the plate contains no reference to the Congress.

Underside: Imperial Porcelain Factory mark of Nicholas II dated 1909; State Porcelain Factory mark dated 1921; "Po ris. Shchekatikhinoi" (from a design by Shchekotikhina); initials Ek. B. for factory painter Ekaterina Bol'sheva.

Diam.: 10 in. (25.4 cm)
Illustrated p. 59

Similar objects are illustrated or discussed in: Christie's, Apr. 27, 1990, lot 334; de Tiesenhausen, 1989, pp. 82–84.

**Aleksandra Vasil'evna Shchekotikhina-Pototskaia
Plate called "The Commissar," 1922**

A military commissar in jodhpurs carries his hat and a blue file marked "Delo N." (Dossier no.). The border indentifies the site in gilt lettering as "Petrograd Ploshchad' Uritskogo" (Uritskii Square, Petrograd), now, as before the Revolution, known as Palace Square. The Alexander Column and the General Staff Building are visible behind him. The position of commissar was established during the Civil War by Leon Trotsky, the first head of the Red Army. Attached to military units, they oversaw the political education of the troops and monitored the loyalty of commanding officers, many of whom had been officers in the imperial army. Although the commissars held no place within the military hierarchy, they could override a commanding officer's orders if they suspected him of counterrevolutionary activity. Palace Square was renamed after Moisei Solomonovich Uritskii, a prominent Bolshevik and chairman of the Petrograd Cheka (secret police), who was assassinated in the square in 1918.

Underside: Imperial Porcelain Factory mark of Nicholas II dated 1898; State Porcelain Factory mark dated 1922, numbered 322/3; "Po ris. Shchekotikhinoi" (From a design by Shchekotikhina); monogram of factory painter Ekaterina Iakimovskaia.

Diam.: 8¾ in. (22.2 cm)
Illustrated p. 67

Similar objects are illustrated or discussed in: Alekseev, 1962, p. 66; Andreeva, 1975, p. 167; *Art into Production*, no. 221; Christie's, Oct. 29, 1985, lot 239, and Oct. 6, 1988, lot 278, and Apr. 27, 1990, lot 332; Gollerbakh and Farmakovskii, 1924, ill. opposite p. 66; Lobanov-Rostovsky, 1990, pl. 36; *La Rivoluzione in salotto*, pl. 97; Tolstoi, 1989, p. 147.

Nikolai Mikhailovich Suetin
Cup and saucer, 1923

The surfaces of the cup and saucer are covered with a Suprematist design in orange, yellow, black, and green.

Suetin was studying at the Vitebsk Popular Art Institute (then directed by Marc Chagall) when Kazimir Malevich arrived in September 1919. Malevich's Suprematist painting rejected recognizable objects in favor of intuitively colored geometric forms representing a higher state of consciousness. A group formed around Malevich at the institute with the intent of applying Suprematism as a spatial or graphic art to utilitarian projects such as architecture, textiles, furniture, metalwork, and typography. Tensions among faculty members resulted in the departure of Malevich and several of his students for Petrograd in April 1922. Suetin and Il'ia Grigor'evich Chashnik, Malevich's two most important students, secured positions at the State Porcelain Factory, most likely through the art critic Nikolai Punin, an associate of Malevich who had become influential there. Suetin was appointed artistic director in 1932. Chashnik and Suetin found the white blanks a perfect "canvas" for their designs, and successfully developed utilitarian Suprematist objects. Suprematist porcelain is discussed in: *The Avant-Garde in Russia,* pp. 250–51; Bowlt, 1978; *Kazimir Malevich,* p. 30; and Zhadova, 1982.

Underside (cup): Imperial Porcelain Factory mark of Alexander III dated [18]92; State Porcelain Factory mark dated 1923, numbered 474; "Suprematizm," with emblem of a black square within an open square; "Po ris. Suetina" (From a design by Suetin).
Underside (saucer): Imperial Porcelain Factory mark of Alexander III dated [18]89; State Porcelain Factory mark dated 1923, numbered 474/382; "Suprematizm," with emblem of a black square within an open square; "Po ris. Suetina" (From a design by Suetin).

Height (cup): 2½ in. (6.4 cm)
Diam. (saucer): 5½ in. (14 cm)
Illustrated p. 44

Vasilii Porfir'evich Timorev
Plate, undated

A Sovietized figure of Saint George, the patron saint of Russia, slays a dragon as a red star rises in the background. His shield bears wheat sheaves and a hammer and sickle. The Russian border decoration reads "Kto ne s nami, tot protiv nas" (He who is not with us is against us). This image is related to a 1920 Soviet calendar, in which Leon Trotsky, as a mounted knight, stands in for Saint George (repr. in White, 1988, p. 7). In this image, Trotsky, with—amazingly—a halo in the form of a star, slays a huge snake marked "counterrevolution" and wearing a top hat. This plate is signed, and perhaps dated, on the lower part of the center.

Underside: Obliterated mark; undated State Porcelain Factory mark; mark of Timorev.

Diam.: 13⅛ in. (33.3 cm)
Illustrated p. 37

Vasilii Porfir'evich Timorev
Vase, 1921

The inscriptions on this large vase are rendered in German, Chinese, and Russian. Circling the neck of the vase, they read "Chuan fang pin kung chih lien ho" (Proletarians from all directions, unite) in Chinese, "Proletarier aller Länder vereinigt euch!" (Proletarians of all lands, unite!) in German, and "Trudiashchimsia" (To the workers) in Russian. The pink squares behind the four figures' heads supply the beginning of the Russian inscription around the neck: "Fabriki" (Industrial plants), "Zavody" (Factories), "Voda" (Sea), and "Zemlia" (Land); the entire inscription, then, reads "Industry, factories, sea, [and] land to the workers." An industrial worker, a Red Army man, a sailor, and a peasant hold hands to form an unbroken chain around the vase's surface, symbolically protecting the resources of the nation. This vase represents the unity of the three elements of the proletariat (workers, peasants, and soldiers) necessary for building socialism. Timorev's signature and the date "21.

IX." are visible on a white square near the peasant. The letters A. R. A., scratched into the surface of the underside, may relate to the American Relief Administration and its efforts to help relieve the Volga famine.

Underside: Undated State Porcelain Factory mark; mark of Timorev; roman letters A. R. A.

Height: 19¾ in. (50.2 cm)
Illustrated p. 23

Attributed to Elizaveta Berngardovna Rozendorf formerly attributed to Rudol'f Fedorovich Vil'de
Plate, 1920

This plate refers to the early campaign for literacy in the Soviet Union. The rim is decorated with open and closed books and sheets of paper reading "Uchis' gramote, zhit' legche" (Learn your letters in order to live better). Various tools of literacy (a scroll, two books, and a globe) nearly cover a crossed rake and scythe. The juxtaposition of study materials with agricultural tools may indicate that this plate was directed primarily toward a rural audience. As in most nations, literacy levels were much lower in the countryside. The Soviet government fostered literacy in the cities by organizing classes through the workplaces of citizens. It was more difficult to bring rural residents together for daily classes. The government sponsored posters encouraging peasants to study on their own, and Soviet propaganda artists attempted to make home study an attractive idea by connecting literacy with increased wealth. They argued that the newly literate, able to read texts on agronomy, animal husbandry, or veterinary medicine, were likely to have healthier and more abundant crops and animals. Such images were criticized for suggesting that the accumulation of wealth was the primary benefit of literacy (see White, 1988, p. 116).

Underside: Obliterated Imperial Porcelain Factory mark; State Porcelain Factory mark dated 1920.

Diam.: 8½ in. (21.6 cm)
Illustrated p. 40

Similar objects are illustrated or discussed in: Christie's, Apr. 24, 1991, lot 66; Sysoeva, 1989, p. 116.

Rudol'f Fedorovich Vil'de
Plate, 1921

This scalloped plate is decorated with a blue gear whose spokes bear the command "Derzai!" (Be brave!) in gold capitals. The spaces between the spokes read "Eshchë raz i vsegda" (Again and always), with a gold hammer and sickle against a red star. This plate, made in 1921, exhorts the Soviet viewer—who, probably, had survived the deprivation and terror of World War I, the Revolution, and the Civil War—to remain courageous in the face of the country's continuing problems. With most military threats removed, the country faced rebuilding an economy battered by years of neglect.

Underside: Partially obliterated Imperial Porcelain Factory mark of Nicholas II; State Porcelain Factory mark dated 1921. The unusually large and transparent Imperial mark may indicate that this is a later copy.

Diam.: 8⅞ in. (22.5 cm)
Illustrated p. 36

Similar objects are illustrated or discussed in: Andreeva, 1971, pl. 141; *Art into Production,* p. 30; Guerman, 1979, p. 355; Lansere, 1974, pl. 29; Sotheby's, Dec. 6, 1989, lot 447, and Nov. 30, 1990, lot 191; Tolstoi, 1989, p. 186.

Attributed to Rudol'f Fedorovich Vil'de
Plate, 1921

Much of the early visual propaganda produced by Russian artists simply commemorated the October Revolution. Artists' committees decorated the streets, squares, and buildings of major cities to serve as backdrops for parades and spectacles on the anniversary and other important dates. The State Porcelain Factory often created designs honoring each passing year; this plate, like cat. no. 13, celebrates the fourth anniversary of the Revolution. A decorative blue sickle and a hammer surround a floral bouquet in the center. The rim reads "Rossiia 1917-1921" (Russia) in red and black lettering that closely resembles the distinctive, woodcutlike style Chekhonin developed in book design in the teens and twenties. Nina Lobanov-Rostovsky suggests that the handle of the sickle may conceal the coat of arms of the imperial or another aristocratic family, and that the plate may have been intended as a gift.

Underside: Imperial Porcelain Factory mark of Nicholas II dated 1912; State Porcelain Factory mark dated 1921.

Diam.: 9¼ in. (23.5 cm)
Illustrated p. 58

Similar objects are illustrated or discussed in: Lobanov-Rostovsky, 1990, pl. 49; *Russische Kunst*, pl. 22.

Rudol'f Fedorovich Vil'de
Plate, 1921

A red banner reading "Pobeda trudiashchikh 25 Okt." (The victory of the workers of October 25th) flies above a hammer, sickle, and wheat sheaf in the center. The cobalt-blue border is decorated with etched gold foliage and various tools (a hammer, a scythe, an axe, and a gear) in silver, now oxidized.

Underside: State Porcelain Factory mark dated 1921.

Diam.: 9½ in. (24.1 cm)
Illustrated p. 29

Similar objects are illustrated or discussed in: Alekseev, 1962, p. 22; Andreeva, 1975, p. 102; Lansere, 1974, pl. 5; *Das Leben zur Kunst Machen*, pl. 35; Lobanov-Rostovsky, 1989, p.132, and 1990, pl. 48; *La Rivoluzione in salotto*, pl. 11.

Rudol'f Fedorovich Vil'de
Plate, 1922

The slogan "Da Zdravstvuet IX S'ezd" (Long live the Ninth Congress [of the Soviets]) encircles the border along with a large blue and purple sickle and flowers. A large hammer, crossed by a section of a gear and surrounded by leaves, decorates the reserve.

Underside: Obliterated mark; State Porcelain Factory mark dated 1922, numbered 27/9. Diam.: 9⅜ in. (23.9 cm)
Illustrated p. 13

Similar objects are illustrated or discussed in: Lobanov-Rostovsky, 1990, pl. 53.

Rudol'f Fedorovich Vil'de
Plate, 1922

An allegorical figure with a halo in the shape of a red star, representing Labor, carrying a hammer and sickle in one hand, and a banner reading "Spasti Revoliutsiiu, pomoch' golodaiushchim" (Save the Revolution, help the starving), floats above modern factories and a smokestack. The border reads "Proletarii vsekh stran soediniates" (Proletarians of all countries unite). The plate's inscription refers to the 1920–21 famine in the Volga region, which affected 37.5 million people. Signs of famine had been present as early as 1919, but the government had been unwilling to acknowledge or publicize the problem until the summer of 1921, fearing that such information would be used as evidence of incompetence and would fuel political opposition both within and outside of the country. In order to alleviate the desperate situation, the fledgling Soviet government was forced to turn to the same foreign governments with whom it had only recently been at war. Although the American Relief Administration (A. R. A.) provided the majority of famine relief, plates such as this were directed at the residents of Soviet cities, which were relatively well supplied, in order to encourage them to share whatever they had with famine victims in the largely agricultural Volga region.

Underside: Imperial Porcelain Factory mark of

Nicholas II dated 1896; State Porcelain Factory five-year anniversary mark dated 1922, numbered 407/2.

Diam.: 14 in. (35.6 cm)
Illustrated on frontispiece

Similar objects are illustrated or discussed in: Alekseev, 1962, p. 23; Andreeva, 1975, pp. 58, 102.

NUMBER 38

Rudol'f Fedorovich Vil'de
Plate, 1922

The mustard-colored rim is decorated with the Russian inscription "Pobeda trudiashchikhsia 25 Oktiabria" (The workers' victory of the 25th of October) in black lettering. The reserve has a hammer and sickle within a wreath of entwined wheat and cornflowers. On October 25 (November 7), 1917, the Russian Provisional Government, which had taken power after Tsar Nicholas II's February abdication, fell to the forces of the Military-Revolutionary Committee of the Petrograd Soviet. The uprising was apparently timed so that the victory could be announced at the Second Congress of the Soviets.

Underside: Obliterated mark; State Porcelain Factory mark dated 1921.

Diam.: 9¾ in. (24.8 cm)
Illustrated p. 26

Similar objects are illustrated or discussed in: Alekseev, 1962, p. 22; Lobanov-Rostovsky, 1990, pl. 51; Tolstoi, 1989, p. 191.

NUMBER 39

Attributed to Petr Vladimirovich Vychegzhanin
Plate, 1922

The large initials for R.S.F.S.R. (Russian Soviet Federal Socialist Republic), the largest republic of the Soviet Union, have been rendered in a floral and linear pattern that covers the center. Foliage, red and yellow floral buds, and a single, large purple flower in full bloom are scat-

tered around the border.

Nina Lobanov-Rostovsky (1990) has cast serious doubt on Vychegzhanin's design of any State Porcelain Factory plates on the basis of his age at the time of their creation. Vychegzhanin was one of the two stepsons of factory director Sergei Chekhonin, and she believes that Chekhonin may have attributed work to him in order to substantiate the claim that he was a factory employee, thus securing more food coupons for his family.

Underside: Undated Imperial Porcelain Factory mark of Alexander III numbered 744894; State Porcelain Factory mark dated 1922, numbered 257/1.

Diam.: 9¾ in. (24.8 cm)
Illustrated p. 56

Similar objects are illustrated or discussed in: Andreeva 1975, p. 199; *Art into Production*, p. 43; Guerman, 1979, p. 343; Lobanov-Rostovsky, 1990, p. 72; Makarov, 1984, p. 61; Tolstoi, 1980, p. 8, and 1989, p. 152.

NUMBER 40

Unattributed
Plate, 1921

The plate features a maroon five-pointed Soviet star decorated with a gilt hammer and sickle. The spaces between the points of the star are covered by floral forms and inscribed "Proletarii vsekh stran soediniates'" (Workers of all countries unite). The scalloping of the rim decoration and the sharp lettering style are very unusual in State Porcelain Factory production.

Underside: Imperial Porcelain Factory mark of Nicholas II dated 1898; State Porcelain Factory mark dated 1921; initials L. G. for factory painter Liubov' Nikolaevna Gaush.

Diam.: 9½ in. (24.1 cm)
Illustrated p. 48

Similar objects are illustrated or discussed in: Sotheby's, Nov. 30, 1990, lot 186.

Unattributed
Plate, 1922

The border is inscribed with the phrase "25 Okt. 1917–1922" in honor of the fifth anniversary of Soviet rule. The roman numeral V crests the center, in which a clean-shaven worker in foundry overalls and a bearded peasant, with their respective hammer and plow, join hands across the worker's anvil. A red star rises like a sun above a horizon of hills.

Underside: Imperial Porcelain Factory mark of Nicholas II dated 1899; State Porcelain Factory five-year anniversary mark dated 1922, numbered 411/3.

Diam.: 9⅞ in. (25.1 cm)
Illustrated p. 81

A similar plate appears in Christie's Apr. 26, 1989, lot 253.

Unattributed
Plate, 1922

The black trelliswork on the border has been embellished with foliage and an orange banner reading "Um ne terpit nevoli" (The mind cannot tolerate slavery). The reserve has a silhouette of Grigorii Zinov'ev, one of the leaders of the Bolshevik Party and the first president of the Third International. The coloring and style of this plate suggest that its design was derived from a dinner service for the Order of Saint George the Victorious created at the Imperial Porcelain Factory during Catherine II's reign. The service was decorated with the black and orange attributes of the order's medals, and was used at a banquet for its members held annually at the Winter Palace on the feast day of Saint George. Zinov'ev joined the opposition against Stalin and was removed from the presidency of the Comintern and other offices in 1926 and 1927. He was eventually accused, falsely, of participation in a conspiracy to murder Sergei Kirov, head of the Communist Party in Leningrad, and was executed after confessing.

Underside: Obliterated Imperial Porcelain Factory mark of Nicholas II; State Porcelain Factory mark dated 1922, numbered 51/2.

Diam.: 9¾ in. (24.8 cm)
Illustrated p. 19

Similar objects are illustrated or discussed in: Andreeva, 1975, p. 109; *Art into Production*, p. 43; Christie's, Apr. 27, 1990, lot 328, and Oct. 10, 1990, lot 316.

Unattributed
Cup, c. 1924/28

This plain, heavy coffee cup is decorated with a design after the eighth plate of Natan Al'tman's (1920) album of drawings of Lenin from life. The drawing is the only decoration on the cup. Although the drawing of Lenin was published in 1920, the cup was probably not produced for several years. Nina Tumarkin (1983) has noted that the deification of Lenin in visual imagery did not begin until after his death in 1924. Images of him in various guises—as a child, as a student, and as a leader—were widely produced until around 1926 or 1928, when his image was supplanted by that of Stalin.

Underside: Undated State Porcelain Factory mark.

Height: 3¾ in. (9.5 cm)
Illustrated p. 11

Similar objects are illustrated or discussed in: Christie's, Oct. 5, 1989, lot 349.

K.K.

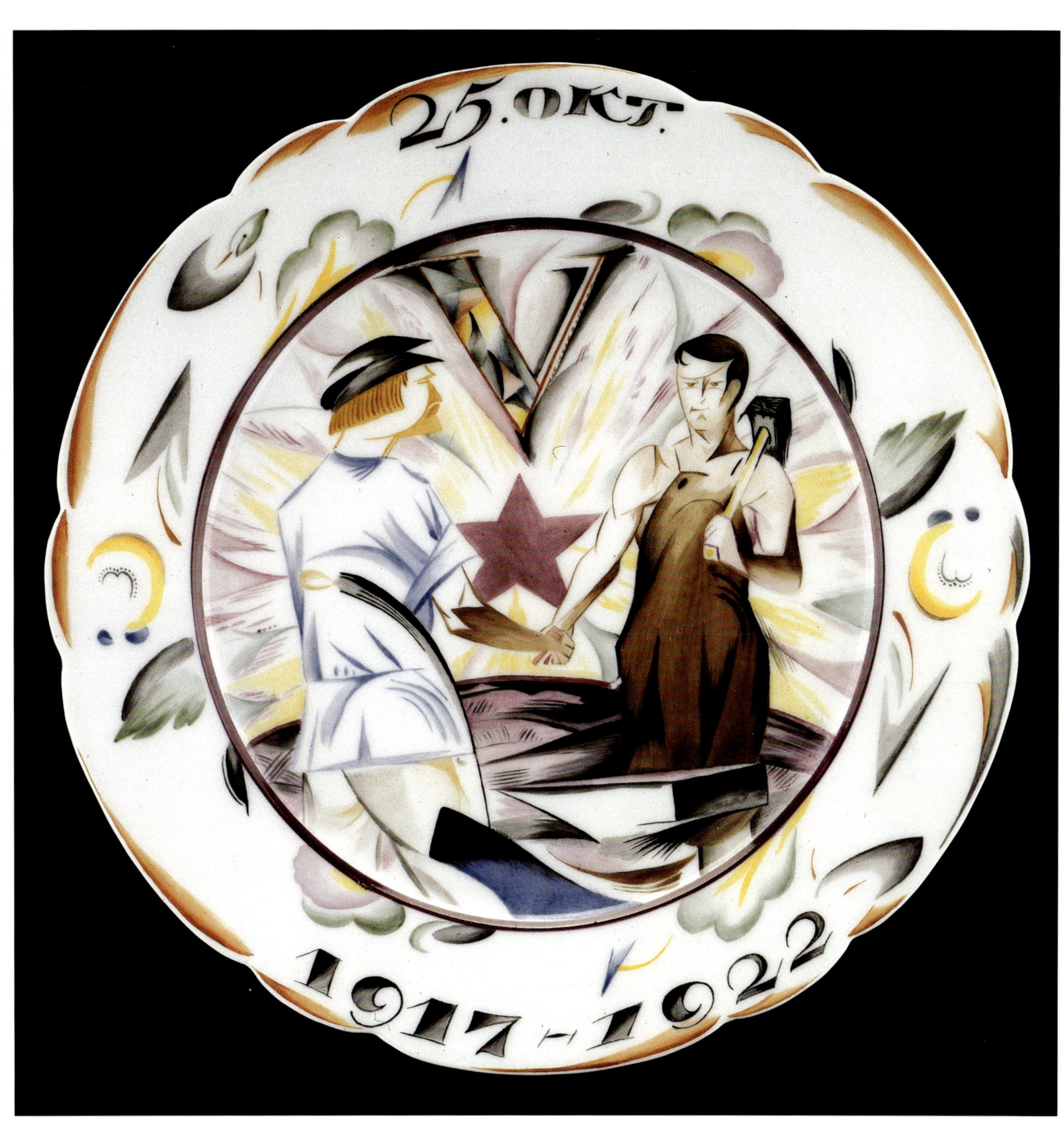

NO. 41

Plate, 1922

Catalogue Sources

Abramova, S. A., ed. *Sovetskii farfor* (Moscow, 1927), including articles by A. V. Lunacharskii, S. Troinitskii, V. V. Filatov, S. A. Trantseev.

Alekseev, B. *Sovetskii khudozhetsvennyi farfor, 1918–1923* (Moscow, 1962).

Al'tman, Natan. *Lenin, Risunki* (Petrograd, 1920).

Andreeva, Lidiia. "Sovetskii agitatsionnyi farfor," in Speranskaia, 1971, pp. 199–213.

———. *Sovetskii farfor 1920–1930 gody* (Moscow, 1975).

———. "Soviet Ceramics," in *Art into Production*, pp. 8–13.

Art Born of the October Revolution/Iskusstvo, rozhdennoe Oktiabrem, booklet from the State Order of Lenin Museum, Moscow (n. d., n. pag.).

Art into Production: Soviet Textiles, Fashion and Ceramics, 1917–1935, exh. cat. Oxford Museum of Modern Art (1984).

Atterbury, Paul. "A Revolutionary Collection," *Ceramics* [U.K.] 2 (Feb.–Mar. 1986), pp. 57–63.

Avanguardia Russa: dalle collezioni private sovietiche origini e percorso 1904–1934, exh. cat. Palazzo Reale, Milan (1988).

The Avant-Garde in Russia, 1910–1930: New Perspectives, exh. cat. Los Angeles County Museum of Art (Cambridge, Mass., 1980).

Baranova, Olga. *Kouskovo: Musée de la céramique et proprieté du XVIIIe siècle* (Leningrad, 1983).

Bowlt, John E. "Malevich and his Students," *Soviet Union/Union Soviétique* 5, no. 2 (1978), pp. 256–86.

———. *The Silver Age: Russian Art of the Early Twentieth Century and the "World of Art" Group* (Newtonville, Mass., 1982).

Christie's, London. *Russian and Greek Icons and Russian Works of Art* (Oct. 29, 1985).

———. *Imperial and Post-Revolutionary Russian Art* (Oct. 6, 1988).

———. *Icons, Russian Paintings and Works of Art* (Apr. 26, 1989).

———. *Imperial and Post-Revolutionary Russian Art* (Oct. 5, 1989).

———. *Imperial and Post-Revolutionary Russian Art* (Oct. 10, 1990).

———. *Icons, Russian Paintings, Prints, Books and Works of Art* (Apr. 27, 1990).

———. *Icons, Russian Pictures, Avant-Garde Books and Works of Art* (Apr. 24, 1991).

Danilov, T. "Agitatsionnyi farfor (20ye gody)," *Dekorativnoe iskusstvo* 11 (1967), pp. 23–26.

Dan'ko, Elena. "Sovetskii farfor (Soviet China)," *Zhizn' iskusstva* no. 17 (1137), 1929, trans. and excerpted in Zhadova, 1982, pp. 331–32.

———. *Khudozhestvennyi farfor. Gosudarstvennyi farforovyi zavod im. M. V. Lomonosova*, exh. cat. Museum of the State Porcelain Factory, Leningrad (1938).

De Tiesenhausen, Alexis. "Propaganda in Porcelain," *Country Life* 183, no. 46 (Nov. 16, 1989), pp. 82–84.

Efros, A., and N. Punin. *S. Chekhonin* (Moscow-Leningrad, 1924).

Emme, B. N. *Sovetskii khudozhestvennyi farfor* (Moscow-Leningrad, 1950).

———. *Gosudarstvennyi Russkii muzei*, exh. cat. Russian Museum, Leningrad (1937).

Filippov, A. V., ed. *Khudozhestvennoe oformlenie massovoi posudy* (Moscow-Leningrad, 1932).

Franzke, Irmela. "Russisches Porzellan mit Suprematistischem Dekor im Badischen Landesmuseum Karlsruhe," *Keramos* no. 78 (Oct. 1977).

———. "Zum Dekorationsstil russischer Porzellane im ersten Jahrzehnt nach der Oktober-Revolution," *Jahrbuch der Staatlichen Kunstsammlungen in Baden-Wurttenberg* 12 (1975), pp. 195–202.

Franzke, Irmela, et al. *Russisches Porzellan, 1895–1935* (Heidelberg, 1992).

Gollerbach, Eric. *La Porcelaine de la manufacture de l'état* (Moscow, 1922).

Gollerbakh, E. F., and M. V. Farmakovskii. *Porcelaine de l'art Russe* (Moscow, 192?).

Gollerbakh, E. F., and M. V. Farmakovskii, eds. *Russkii khudozhestvennyi farfor: Sbornik statei o gosudarstvennom farforovom zavode* (Leningrad, 1924).

Guerman, Mikhail. *Art of the October Revolution* (Leningrad and New York, 1979).

Kazimir Malevich, 1878–1935, exh. cat. Stedelijk Museum, Amsterdam (1989).

Kogan, P., et al. *Exposition internationale des arts décoratifs et industriels modernes* [Paris], *Union des Républiques Soviétiques Socialistes,* exh. cat. (Moscow, 1925).

Lansere, A. K. "Agitatsionnyi farfor (iz istorii gosudarstvennogo zavoda im. M. V. Lomonosova)," *Dekorativnoe Iskusstvo,* vol. 11 (1967), pp. 9–12.

———. *Sovetskii farfor. Iskusstvo Leningradskogo gosudarstvennogo farforogo zavoda imeni M. V. Lomonosova/Soviet Porcelain: Art of the M. V. Lomonosov State Porcelain Factory, Leningrad* (Leningrad, 1974), short summary of text in English.

Das Leben zur Kunst Machen: Arbeiten auf Papier von Frauen der russischen Avantgarde; Stoffe und Porzellen aus der jungen Sowjetunion, exh. cat. Helmhaus, Zurich (1989).

Lianda, Natalia. "Sergei Chekhonin," *Soviet Union/Union Soviétique 7,* pts. 1–2 (1980), pp. 157–69.

Lobanov-Rostovsky, Nina. "Soviet Propaganda Porcelain," *Journal of the Decorative and Propaganda Arts,* Winter 1989.

———. *Revolutionary Ceramics: Soviet Porcelain, 1917–1927* (New York, 1990).

Lukomski, Georges. "Neues Russisches Porzellan," *Dekorative Kunst* no. 28 (May 1925), pp. 201–05.

Makarov, *Sovetskoe dekorativnoe iskusstvo, 1917–1945* (Moscow, 1984).

Noskovich, V. *Aleksandra Shchekotikhina-Pototskaia* (Leningrad, 1959).

Paris–Moscou, 1910–1930, exh. cat. Centre Georges Pompidou, Paris (1979).

Pushkarev, V. A. *Sovetskii khudozhestvennyi farforovyi zavod im. M. V. Lomonosova* (Leningrad, 1961).

Raeburn, Walter. "Pottery and Propaganda," *Apollo,* Jan. 1966, pp. 56–61.

La Rivoluzione in salotto: Porcellane sovietiche, 1917–1930, exh. cat. Comune di Venezia (Milan, 1988).

Russische Kunst, exh. cat. Galerie Michael Pabst, Munich (1989).

Sotheby's, London. *Russian Pictures, Works of Art and Icons* (Dec. 5–6, 1989).

———. *Icons, Russian Pictures and Works of Art* (Nov. 30, 1990).

Speranskaia, E. A., et al., eds. *Agitatsionno-massovoe iskusstvo pervykh let Oktiabria: Materialy i issledovania* (Moscow, 1971).

Sysoeva, T., ed. *Agitatsionnyi farfor,* booklet from the Perm [U.S.S.R.] Museum (1989).

Tolstoi, Vladimir. *Art décoratif soviétique, 1917–1937* (Paris, 1989).

Tolstoi, V., ed. *Farfor, faians, steklo, 1917–1932. Sovetskoe dekorativnoe iskusstvo. Materialy i dokumenty* (Moscow, 1980).

"Tschechonin" (unsigned), *Die Kunst,* June 1929, pp. 221–24.

Tumarkin, Nina. *Lenin Lives! The Lenin Cult in Soviet Russia* (Cambridge, 1983).

White, Steven. *The Bolshevik Poster* (New Haven, Conn., 1988).

Zhadova, L. *Malevich: Suprematism and Revolution in Russian Art, 1910–1930* (New York, 1982).

K.K.

Biographies of State Porcelain Factory Designers

Only artists whose work is represented in the Tuber Collection are discussed here. The entries are intended only to suggest the salient events of their careers.

Mikhail Mikhailovich Adamovich 1884–1947

1907 Graduates with honors from the Stroganov School of Art and Industrial Design and receives a scholarship to study the decorative arts in Italy for two years. **1914** Commissioned by Greek government to produce the mosaic designs for the tomb of King George I. **1918–19** Works as a designer at the State Porcelain Factory. **1920–21** Serves in the Red Army. **1921–23** Resumes work at the State Porcelain Factory. **1922** Exhibits with *Mir iskusstva* group. **1924** Exhibits with the Association of Artists of Revolutionary Russia. (AKhRR) and *Mir iskusstva*. **1924–27** Works at the Volkhov Ceramic Factory in Novgorod. **1925** Receives a medal at the Paris International Exposition of Decorative and Industrial Arts. **1928–34** Works at the Dulevo Ceramics Factory in Moscow. **1934–47** Paints decorative works in Moscow public buildings

Natan Isaevich Al'tman 1889–1970

1902/03–07 Studies at the Odessa Art School under Kostandi. **1910–12** Studies at Mariia Vasilieva's Free Russian Academy in Paris. **1910–18** Contributes to many Russian avant-garde exhibitions, such as the "0,10" show. **1912–17** Contributes to the satirical journal *Riab'* (Ripple) in Saint Petersburg. **1918–20** Teaches at SVOMAS, the Free State Art Studios in Petrograd; works for Petrograd IZO Narkompros; designs decoration scheme for Uritskii Square on the First Anniversary of the October Revolution; contributes to the "Exhibition of Paintings and Sculptures by Jewish Artists." **1919** Contributes to the "First State Free Exhibition of Works of Art." **1920** Produces an album of sketches of Lenin done from life. **1922** Contributes to the "First Russian Art Exhibition" in Berlin. **1925** Contributes work to the Paris Exposition. **1929–35** Lives and works in Paris. **1936** Returns to Leningrad.

Veniamin Pavlovich Belkin 1884–1951

1904–05 Studies at the Bolshakov Art School in Moscow. **1906–** Exhibits regularly with *Mir iskusstva* and other societies. **1907–09** Studies in Paris. **1909–** Works in Saint Petersburg contributing caricatures and illustrations to various magazines. **1911** Decorates interior of Stray Dog Cabaret. **1917–18** Visits the Crimea. **1919–21** Works intermittently at the State Porcelain Factory. **1921–46** Teaches painting at the Academy of Arts.

Sergei Vasil'evich Chekhonin 1878–1936

1896–97 Studies drawing at the Society for the Encouragement of the Arts in Saint Petersburg until poverty forces him to leave school. Begins working part-time at the Imperial Porcelain Factory while taking courses at the Baron A. Steiglitz Central School of Technical Design. **1897–1900** Studies painting under Il'ia Repin at Princess Mariia Tenisheva's School. **1904–06** Studies at the Free Studio of Saint Petersburg and at Savva Mamontov's Abramtsevo Ceramic Workshop in Moscow. **1905–06** Publishes cartoons in several satirical socialist journals and is an assistant to the editor of *Zritel'* (Spectator) in Saint Petersburg. **1907** Works at Petr Vaulin's ceramics factory at Kikerino, near Saint Petersburg, and produces decorative majolica panels for the Hotel Metropole in Moscow. **1910** Joins *Mir iskusstva* group and contributes work to their exhibitions until 1924. **1913–18** Named head of the Art Section of the Craft Industries Section of the Ministry of Agriculture. Directs a school for the decorative arts at Rostov-Iaroslavskii. **1918** Elected head of the State Porcelain Factory in Petrograd, a position he holds until 1923. **1920s** Works on designs for the national emblem of the R.S.F.S.R., postage stamps, and paper and silver money. **1923–24** Directs the Volkhov Ceramics Factory, near Novgorod. **1925–27** Becomes director of the State Porcelain Factory, renamed the Lomonosov State Porcelain Factory, for the second time. **1928** Emigrates to Paris, where he works as a designer for Nikolai Baliev's Chauve-Souris cabaret and Vera Nemchinova's Ballet Russes. Exhibits at the Galerie Hirondelle in Paris. **1929** Works for *Vogue* magazine.

Liubov' Nikolaevna Gaush 1877–1943

1889 Begins studying drawing with A. I. Korzykhin. **1909** Graduates from the Society for the Encouragement of the Arts, Saint Petersburg. **After 1909** Studies at the Académie Julien in Paris and exhibits with *Mir iskusstva*. **1919–22** Works at the State Porcelain Factory.

Alisa Rudol'fovna Golenkina 1884–1970

1910 Graduates from the Baron A. Stieglitz Central School of Technical Design. **1919–24** Works as an artist and painter at the State Porcelain Factory.

Zinaida Viktorovna Kobyletskaia 1880–1957

1910 Graduates from the Society for the Encouragement of the Arts in Saint Petersburg. **1910–12** Works as an artist at porcelain factories in France, Denmark, and Sweden. **1912–14** Works as an artist at the Imperial Porcelain Factory. **1918–23** Works as an artist at the State Porcelain Factory. **1925** Receives a Diploma of Honor at Paris Exposition. **1927** Awarded a gold medal in the decorative arts at the International Exhibition of Arts in Monza. **1932–57** Works as an illustrator of botany texts. **1937** Exhibits at the International Exhibition of Arts, Crafts, and Sciences in Paris.

Vladimir Vasil'evich Lebedev 1891–1967

1909 Studies with Aleksandr Titov in Saint Petersburg. **1909–11** Studies with Franz Rubo. **1912–16** Attends the Academy of Arts in Saint Petersburg while studying in the studio of Mikhail Bernstein and Leonid Sherwood. **1911–17** Works as a magazine illustrator. **1918–19** Designs a number of articles for the State Porcelain Factory. **1918–21** Teaches at SVOMAS (State Free Art Studios) in Petrograd. **1920–21** With the poet Mayakovsky, designs propaganda posters for windows of ROSTA (Russian State Telegraph Agency). **1924–45** Produces propaganda posters for the Soviet news agency TASS.

Elizaveta Berngardovna Rozendorf 1898–1984

1919–20 Works at the State Porcelain Factory before moving to Tallinn, Estonia, in the early 1920s. **1940** Moves to Posen, Germany, with her husband. **1945** Flees to Bavaria.

Aleksandra Vasil'evna Shchekotikhina-Pototskaia 1892–1967

1908–15 Studies under Nikolai Roerich and Ivan Bilibin at the Society for the Encouragement of the Arts in Saint Petersburg. **1910** Travels through northern Russia studying decorative arts traditions. **1912–20** Designs costumes for the theater, including productions by Diaghilev and Stravinskii. **1913** Travels to Greece, Italy, and France. While in France, she studies with Maurice Denis. **1915** Begins exhibiting with *Miriskusstva*. **1918–23** Works as an artist at the State Porcelain Factory in Petrograd. **1923–25** With her husband, the artist and book illustrator Ivan Bilibin, and her son, Mstislav, travels through Palestine and Syria, settling in Alexandria. **1925** Returns to Paris for the International Exposition. **1925–36** Lives in Paris; paints Sèvres and Limoges porcelain. **1936** Returns to the Soviet Union. **1936–53** Resumes her position as an artist at the State Porcelain Factory in Leningrad.

Nikolai Mikhailovich Suetin 1897–1954

1918–22 Studies at the Vitebsk Art School with Kazimir Malevich. **1922** Along with Malevich and Il'ia Chashnik, moves to Petrograd, where he works with INKhUKh, the Institute for Artistic Culture, and the State Porcelain Factory. **1928** Designs the interior scheme for the exhibition "Construction of the NKVD" with Anna Leporskaia. **1932** Named Artistic Director of the Lomonosov State Porcelain Factory. **1935** Designs the Suprematist coffin for Malevich upon his death. **1937** Contributes to the interior design of the Soviet Pavilion at International Exhibition of Arts, Crafts, and Sciences in Paris. **1939** Contributes to the interior design of the Soviet Pavilion at the World's Fair in New York.

Vasilii Porfir'evich Timorev 1870–1942

1890 Studies at the Society for the Encouragement of the Arts in Saint Petersburg. **1890–92** Studies in Repin's workshop and at the Academy of Arts in Saint Petersburg. **1918–21** Works as a graphic artist for the publisher Knebel' in Petrograd and at the State Porcelain Factory throughout the twenties.

Rudol'f Fedorovich Vil'de 1868(?)–1942

1894–95 Studies at the workshop of the Prokhovorov Factory (now known as the Three Hills Factory) in Moscow. **1895–99** Studies at the Baron A. Stieglitz Central School of Technical Design. **1899–1902** Stieglitz School sends him on a study tour of France, Germany, and Italy. **1905** Begins working at the Imperial Porcelain Factory as a designer. **1906–30** Heads the Painting Workshop at the Imperial, then the State, Porcelain Factory. **1925** Receives a gold medal for his work at the Paris Exposition. **1938–42** Heads Art Section at the Volkhov Factory.

Petr Vladimirovich Vychegzhanin (Pierre Ino) 1904–?

1919–27 Works as an artist at the State Porcelain Factory. **1928** Emigrates to Paris with Chekhonin (his stepfather) and his mother, Lydia Vychegzhanina, and brother.

K.K.

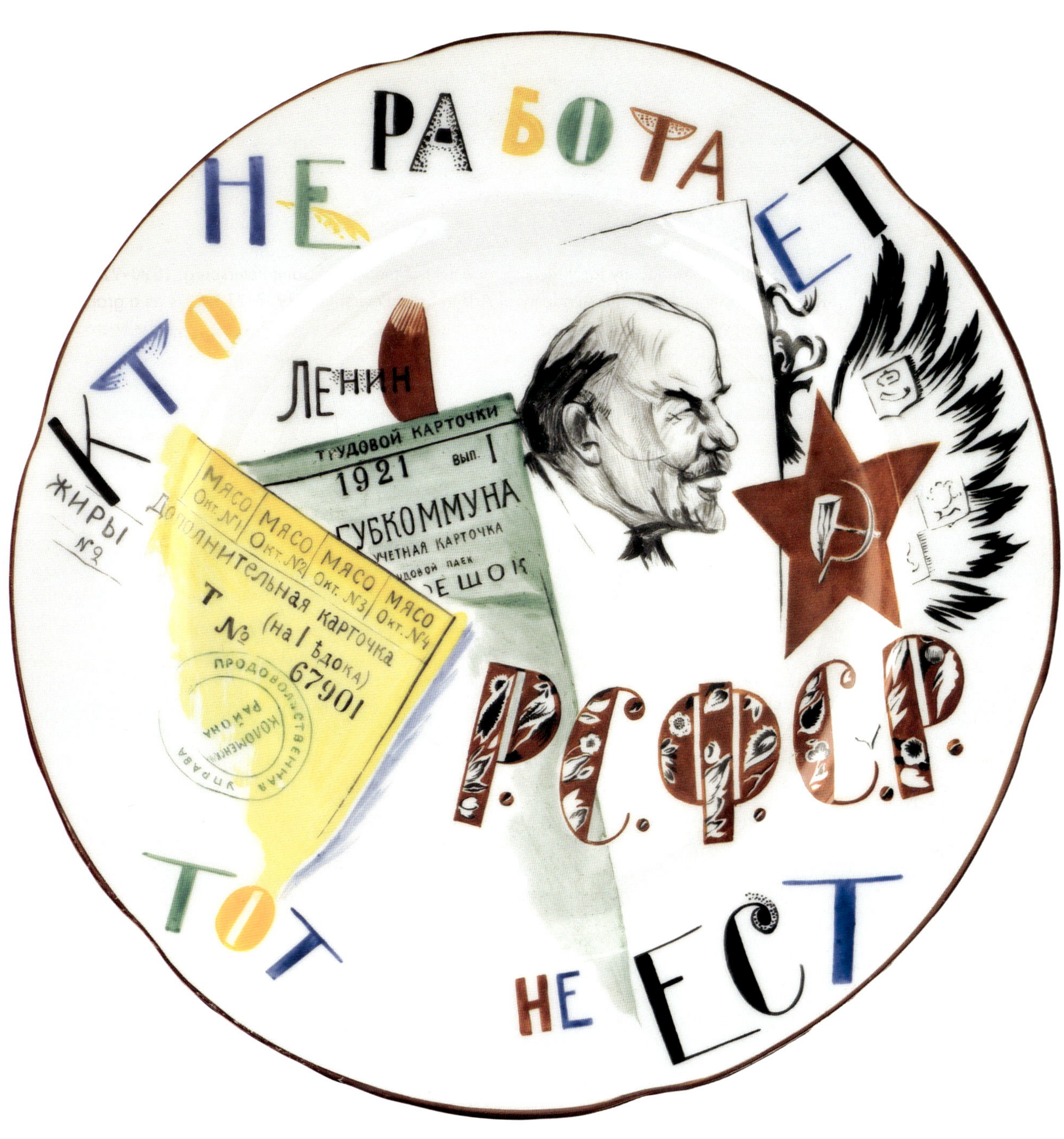
КТО НЕ РАБОТАЕТ ТОТ НЕ ЕСТ
Р.С.Ф.С.Р.
ЛЕНИН
трудовой карточки
1921 вып. I
ГУБКОММУНА
учетная карточка
трудовой паек
ОРЕШОК
ЖИРЫ № 2
МЯСО Окт. №1
МЯСО Окт. №2
МЯСО Окт. №3
МЯСО Окт. №4
Дополнительная карточка
Т № (на I едока)
Т № 67901
ПРОДОВОЛЬСТВЕННАЯ
УПРАВА КОЛОМЕНСКАГО РАЙОНА

Notes on Marks

The undersides of Soviet propaganda plates and other porcelain objects usually bear two layers of factory marks as well as other insignia, including dates, names of painters and designers, and inventory numbers. In the first years of the State Porcelain Factory, blanks from the Imperial Factory were used, and these carry green underglaze initials of the tsars in whose reigns they were fired, usually Nicholas II and Alexander III, as well as the year they were fired. A dark green lozenge or diamond was often painted to obscure the imperial insignia (see figs. 1–2), and the new factory emblems—hammer, sickle, and a section of a cogwheel—were added in various colors and stylizations. Ceramics produced between April and December 1917 may also include the mark of the Provisional Government, a double-headed eagle surrounded by a broken circle.

The phrase "Po ris. [risunku] A. Shchekotikhinoi" along with the initials Ek. B. specifies that the plate was painted by factory artist Ekaterina Bol'sheva after a design by Aleksandra Shchekotikhina (see fig. 3). Painters initialed or, in rare cases, signed their names in overglaze colors. These are of course in Cyrillic, although artists sometimes used roman letters (Shchekotikhina-Pototskaia used A. S.-P.). Some artists used emblems, such as the fleur-de-lys for Timorev. Factory inventory numbers were usually demarked with a cursive N. (roman alphabet) with a number over another number. The year of painting completes the basic information.

Other markings include the Cyrillic for "Suprematism" with the movement's emblem, a black solid square within an open square (see fig. 7). Some plates bear a special mark devised by Chekhonin for the fifth anniversary of the State Porcelain Factory under Narkompros, 1923. Other special marks exist, such as a gold mark for pieces sold in aid of famine victims in 1921, and one celebrating the fifth anniversary of the October Revolution (see fig. 8).

A more comprehensive listing of marks from the State Porcelain Factory, as well as from other Soviet factories, appears in Nina Lobanov-Rostovsky, *Revolutionary Ceramics: Soviet Porcelain, 1917–1927* (New York, 1990), pp. 148–156.

I.W.

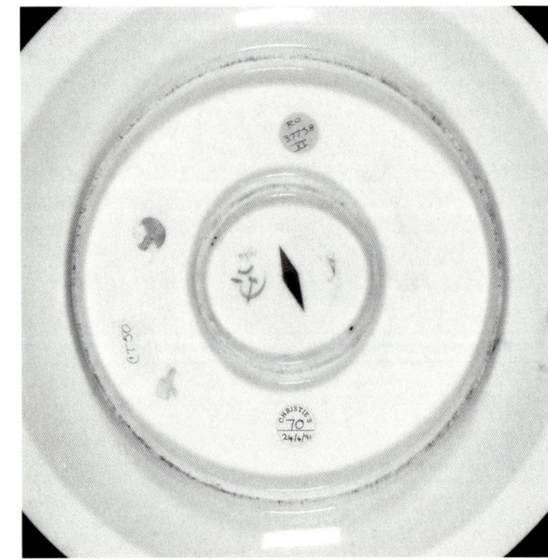

FIGURE 1

Detail of cat. no. 16 (underside)

FIGURE 2

Detail of cat. no. 42 (underside)

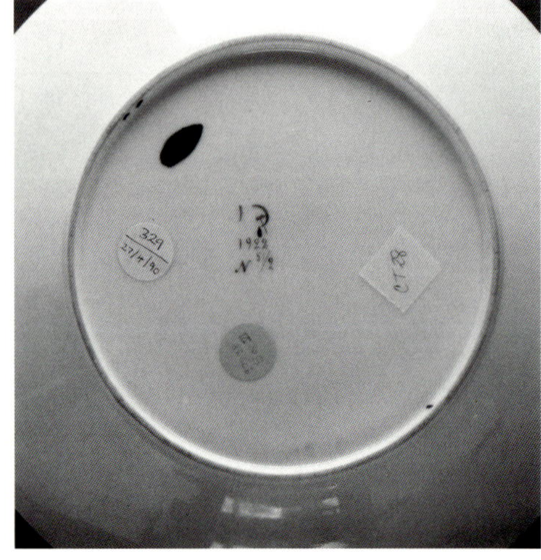

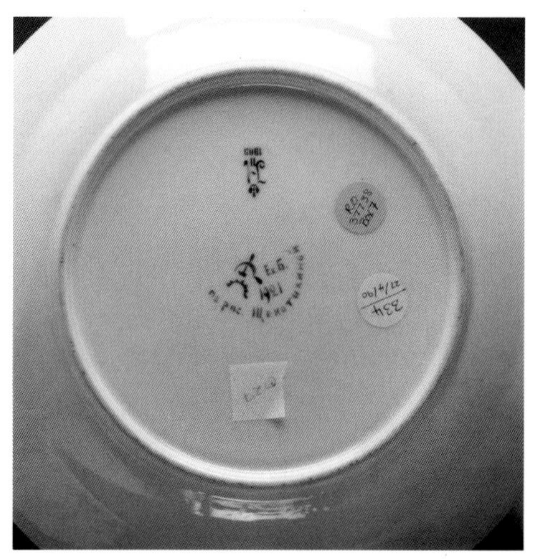

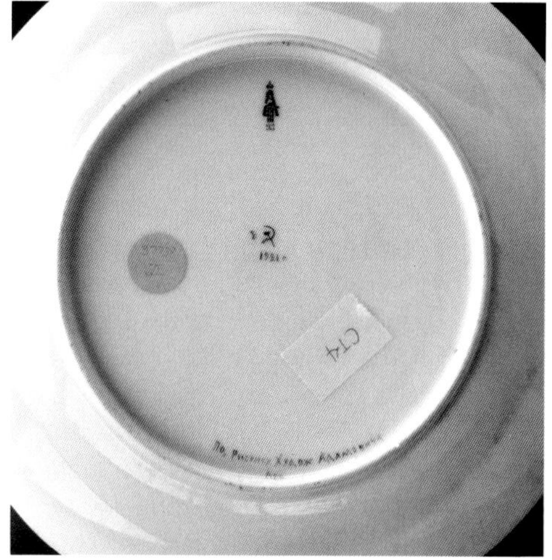

FIGURE 3

Detail of cat. no. 27
(underside)

FIGURE 4

Detail of cat. no. 1
(underside)

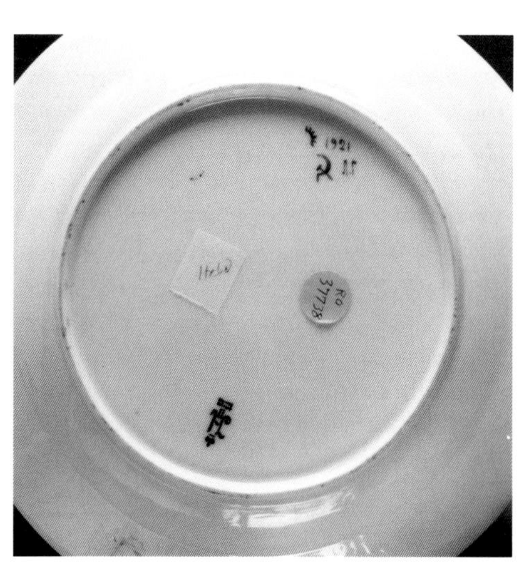

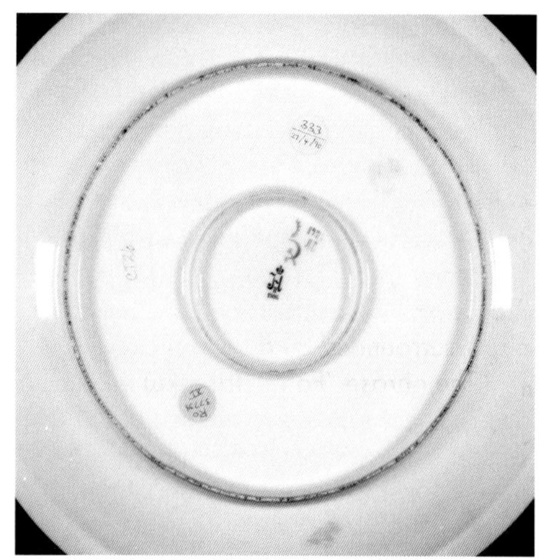

FIGURE 5

Detail of cat. no. 40
(underside)

FIGURE 6

Detail of cat. no. 15
(underside)

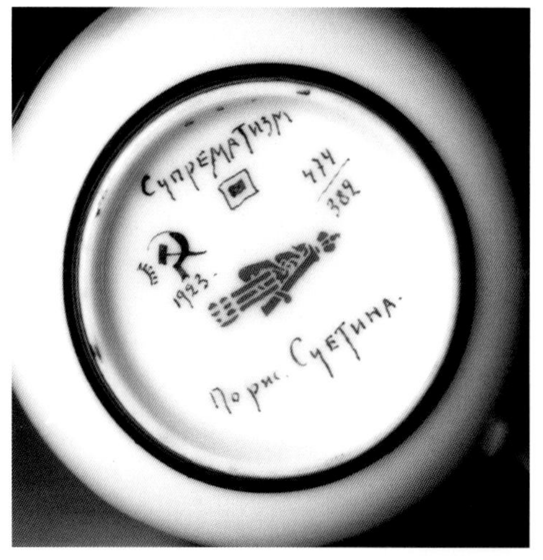

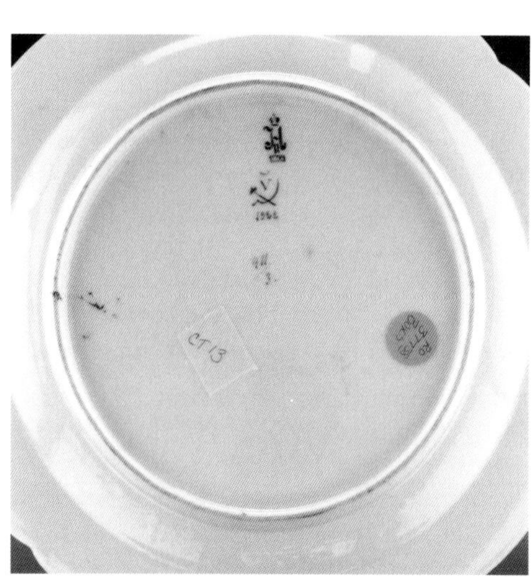

FIGURE 7

Detail of cat. no. 29
(underside)

FIGURE 8

Detail of cat. no. 41
(underside)

Collecting Soviet Porcelain

I have always viewed art collecting as a means of enriching our understanding of history and of expanding our awareness of our own time. My first collecting activity focused on contemporary Soviet art, particularly by Russian artists. It coincided with new possibilities for contact and trade afforded by *perestroika* (restructuring) and *glasnost'* (openness). I was particularly interested in those artists who addressed what they felt were necessary social changes. This contemporary collection provided the basis for my exploration of the propaganda art of the October Revolution.

The new Commonwealth of Independent States has undergone, and is still undergoing, radical changes that are no less momentous than the events of the Revolution in 1917. Many parallels can be drawn between the two periods, most fundamentally that both have seen complete and abrupt transformations of economic and political systems—transformations that cannot occur without immense hardships. Likewise, the artistic activity of both periods has sought to bring about radical shifts. One striking similarity is that both contemporary artists and the propagandists of the early Soviet years have used slogans to advance their ideas. In tumultuous times, artists have frequently found their work active not only in aesthetics, but in the social, economic, and political spheres as well. They have used their creative energies in times of transition to create art that points the way toward the next dominant style.

It is my hope that this collection and catalogue will enhance viewers' understanding of art as propaganda and propaganda as art. The similarities between that era and our own can enable us to explore how artists working in changing situations have used means of expression available to them; and by understanding the art of the propagandists of a past era, we can better appreciate the art of today and tomorrow. As the communist Soviet Union slides into history, we can assess these wares—perhaps the supreme expression of its Revolutionary-period artists—not only for their great beauty, but for what they tell us about the culture that produced them.

I would like to extend my deep appreciation to William and Deborah Struve for providing so much help with this collection. Their knowledge and insights into this area were crucial to my involvement with Soviet porcelain. Ian Wardropper has been of tremendous help in bringing this collection to a wider audience through this catalogue and the exhibition. Karen Kettering has been invaluable in cataloguing and researching these pieces, and Keith Struve has assisted in numerous ways. Lastly, I would like to thank my daughters, Kimberly and Melissa, and my wife, Kay, for their loving support.

Craig H. Tuber
Northfield, Ill.

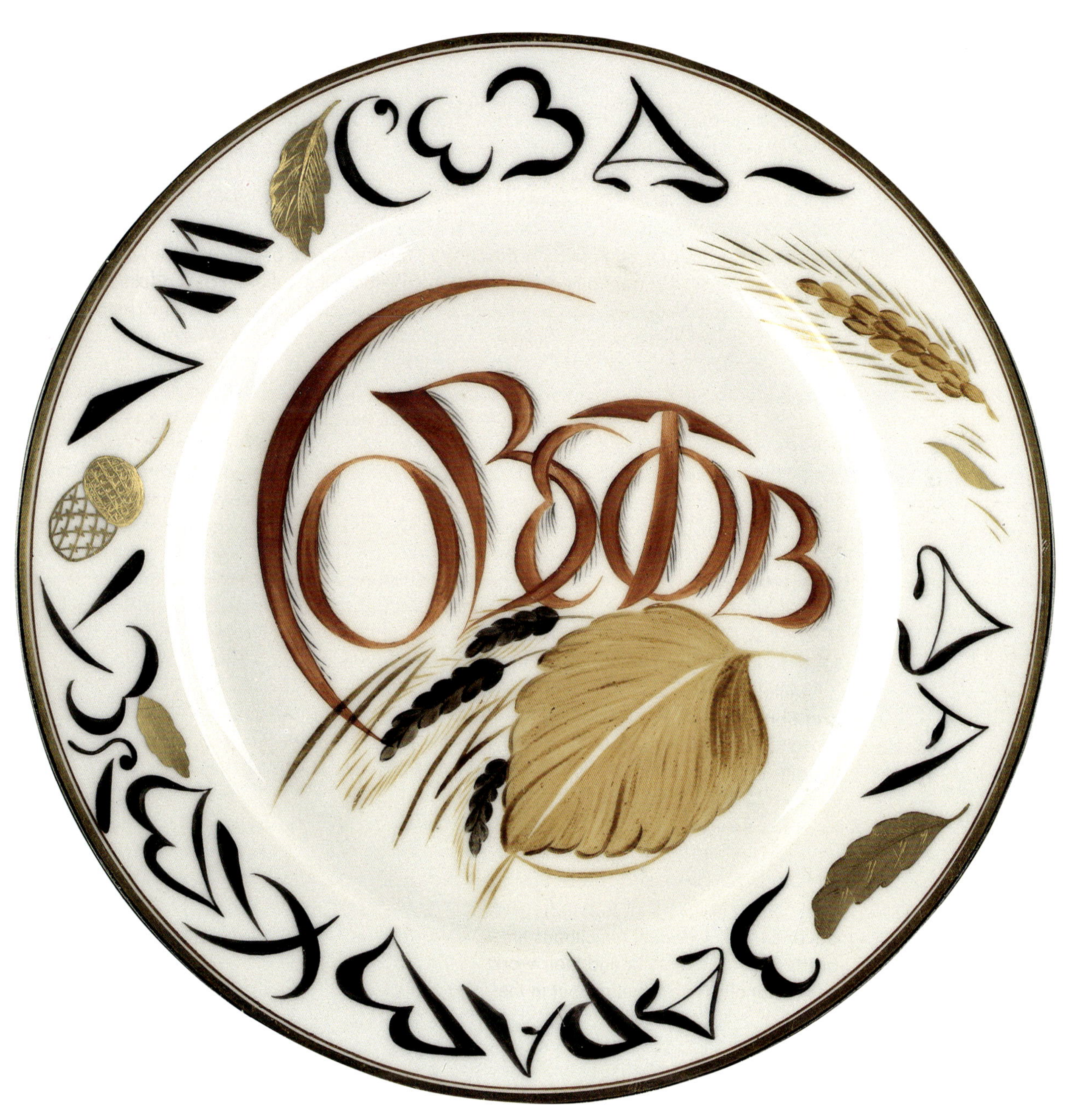

NO. 19

Zinaida Kobyletskaia

Plate, 1921